Word
Pocket Guide

Word
Pocket Guide

Walter Glenn

O'REILLY®

Beijing · Cambridge · Farnham · Köln · Paris · Sebastopol · Taipei · Tokyo

Word Pocket Guide

by Walter Glenn

Copyright © 2003 O'Reilly & Associates, Inc. All rights reserved.
Printed in the United States of America.

Published by O'Reilly & Associates, Inc., 1005 Gravenstein Highway North,
Sebastopol, CA 95472.

O'Reilly & Associates books may be purchased for educational,
business, or sales promotional use. Online editions are also available
for most titles (*safari.oreilly.com*). For more information, contact our
corporate/institutional sales department: (800) 998-9938 or
corporate@oreilly.com.

Editors:	Tim O'Reilly and Nancy Kotary
Production Editor:	Brian Sawyer
Cover Designer:	Emma Colby
Interior Designer:	David Futato

Printing History:

November 2002:   First Edition

0-596-00445-1
[C]   [10/03]

Contents

Part II. Word Tasks

Part III.   Word Reference

Part IV. Word Resources

Word Pocket Guide

Introduction

This Pocket Guide is a quick reference guide to the most recent versions of Microsoft Word—Word 97, 2000, and 2002. It is useful for both new and experienced users of Word, and is put together in the following way:

- Part 1 provides an overview of the most important concepts for working in Word. These are concepts that will make any Word user more efficient and lend a deeper understanding to some of Word's quirks.

- Part 2 is filled with specific tasks covering every aspect of the program, categorized for easy reference. While it is designed primarily as a reference, you can learn a lot about Word from browsing through the tasks.

- Part 3 contains a number of reference tables so that you can easily look up things like keyboard shortcuts, regular expressions, and common file locations.

- Part 4 lists several online resources, add-in tools, and other books that you may find useful.

Conventions Used in This Book

The following typographical conventions are used in this book:

Italic

> Indicates new terms, URLs, filenames, file extensions, directories, and program names. For example, a path in the filesystem will appear as *C:\Program Files\Microsoft Office*.

`Constant width`

> Shows the contents of files, commands and options, or the output from commands.

`Constant width italic`

> Shows typed text that should be replaced with user-supplied values.

Variable lists

> The variable lists throughout Part 2 of this book present tasks as the answer to a "How do I . . ." question (e.g., "How do I mark text other than a heading as a table of contents entry?").

Menus/Navigation

> Menus and their options are referred to in the text as File → Open, Tools → Language → Thesaurus, and so on. Arrows are also used to signify a navigation path when using window options; for example, Tools → Options → View → Bookmarks means that you would open the Tools menu, select the Options command, switch to the View tab, and select the Bookmarks option on that tab.

Pathnames

> Pathnames are used to show the location of a file or application in Windows Explorer. Folders are separated by a backward slash. For example, if you see something like, " . . . default location is *C:\Program Files\Microsoft Office*" in the text, that means the default location of the file being discussed is in the Microsoft Office subfolder of the Program Files folder.

Menu symbols

> When looking at the menus for any application, you will see some symbols associated with keyboard shortcuts for a particular command. For example, to open a document in Microsoft Word, you could go to the File menu and select Open (File → Open), or you could issue the keyboard shortcut, Ctrl-O.

NOTE

Indicates a tip, suggestion, or general note.

WARNING

Indicates a warning or caution.

 In Part 2, we've highlighted some of the especially cool or useful tips for you in these boxes. Even Word experts might learn a thing or two, or get a reminder about an old favorite trick.

In Part 2, the following icons appear in the margin next to the task:

02+

This icon represents features available in Word 2002 and newer versions. Word 97 and Word 2000 do not incorporate these features.

00+

This icon represents features available in Word 2000 and newer versions. Word 97 does not incorporate these features.

PART I

Understanding Word

The first part of this book covers the principal functions of Word. The intent of this part is to help new users hit the ground running and to provide experienced users with a keener understanding of why Word works (and sometimes doesn't work) the way it does.

This part of the book covers:

- The Word Interface
- Template and Document Files
- How a Document Works
- Formatting
- Shortcut Menus
- What Word Tries to Do for You

NOTE

For the most part, users of Word 97 and 2000 should find that the information in this chapter applies to those versions too. We have indicated areas where a feature is specific to Word 2002.

The Word Interface

The basic Word interface (Figure 1) has not changed much throughout its many versions, though some features have changed and much of the underlying technology has been overhauled.

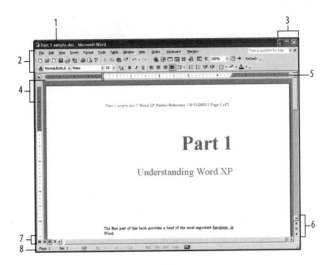

Figure 1. The Word 2002 interface

Figure 1 shows the important elements of the Word 2002 interface. In this list, the numbered items correspond to elements in the figure.

1. *Title Bar.* This bar shows the name of the document and the document's state. For example, if you open multiple windows of the same document (using Window → New Window), Word labels the documents *:1* (the original), *:2*, and so on. If a document is opened as read-only, this designation appears in parentheses beside the document name.

2. *Command Bars.* Menus and toolbars are both called command bars in Word, and their differences are only skin-deep. You can add buttons, commands, and even submenus to any command bar (the technique is covered in Part 2). In Word 2000 and 2002, a feature named *adaptive menus* is enabled by default, causing Word to show only the basic commands (as decided by Microsoft) and the most frequently used commands on both menus

and toolbars, unless you click an extra button to show the rest. You can turn this feature off using Tools → Customize → Options → Always Show Full Menus.

3. *Window Controls*. These controls work a bit differently depending on whether you are using a single or multiple document interface. In the single document interface, a separate window is displayed for each Word document and each document has its own taskbar button. In the multiple document interface, all documents are shown in one master Word window.

- In the single document interface, the Minimize, Maximize, and Close buttons on the title bar affect only the active document, unless only one document is open at the time. In that case, a separate Close Window button is added to the far right of the menu bar. Click it to close the document, but leave Word itself open. Use the regular Close button on the title bar to close both the document and Word.

- In the multiple document interface, the Minimize, Maximize, and Close buttons on the title bar affect the master Word window and all documents open inside it. Separate Minimize, Maximize, and Close buttons are added to each document window.

NOTE

By default, Word 2002 uses the single document interface introduced in Word 2000 (in which a separate window and taskbar button are displayed for each open document). Switch to a multiple document interface by going to Tools → Options → View → Windows in Taskbar. Word 97 offers only the multiple document interface.

---

4. *Rulers*. Two rulers (horizontal and vertical) control the margins and indentation of text in a document. The horizontal ruler (Figure 2) appears directly above the main document window in all of Word's views except for

Outline View. The vertical ruler appears to the left and only in Print Layout View. For the most part, the vertical and horizontal rulers behave the same way, except that the vertical ruler does not feature tabs.

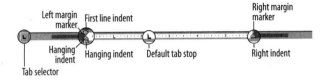

Figure 2. Rulers control tabs, indentation, and margins

Click the tab selector to cycle through the available tab types. Left, center, and right tabs describe how text is aligned on the tab. Decimal tabs align numbers on the decimal point. Bar tabs create vertical display lines. Indents are used to control the placement of first line and hanging indents (which you can also do by dragging the ones already on the ruler). Once you select a tab type, click anywhere on the ruler to place a tab.

Drag the light grey dividers (called margin markers) between the white space and dark grey space on the ruler to adjust the printable margin of the page.

5. *Screen Split Handle.* Double-click this handle (or drag it down) to split the document window into two separate panes, allowing you two views of the same document. Changes made in one pane appear instantly in the other and you can drag selections between panes to move them. Double-click the handle again (or drag it all the way to the top) to close the extra pane.

6. *Browse Object.* This browses through different objects in a document. Click Select Browse Object (the round button) to specify how you want to browse. You can browse fields, endnotes, footnotes, comments, sections, pages, goto and find selections, edits, headings, graphics, or

tables. Once you select a browse object, use the double-arrow Next and Previous buttons to jump between objects.

7. *View Buttons*. These buttons provide fast access to Word's four primary views:

   - *Normal* provides a larger workspace, but you must rely on the status bar to see where you are in the document. One plus to working in Normal view is that page and section breaks are more visible, represented by a horizontal line and text indicating the type of break.

   - *Web Layout* shows any background color or graphic (Format → Background) added to the page and shows the position of text and graphics as they should appear in a web browser. In Word 97, this view is called the Online Layout view, but works pretty much the same way.

   - *Print Layout* adds an extra vertical ruler on the left side of the page and allows you to see the physical edges of the paper, a major help in laying out a document and monitoring pagination.

   - *Outline* displays the document as a hierarchical list of headings and supporting paragraph text. Use this view for planning and structuring document headings.

8. *Status Bar*. Word's status bar (Figure 3) shows the location of the current view in a document (by page) and the location of the insertion point (by section number, page count, line, column, and distance from the left margin).

Current view location	Insertion point location	Background activity indicators

Figure 3. The status bar shows where you are and what Word is doing in the background

The status bar also indicates certain settings and shows when Word is performing background tasks. REC indicates that Word is recording a macro, TRK that the track changes feature is enabled, EXT that the extended double-click option is on, and OVR that overtype is enabled. Icons also appear on the status bar from time to time that show when Word is performing background operations such as repagination, spell-checking, and saving.

NOTE

Double-click the REC, TRK, EXT, and OVR icons to toggle the selection on or off.

Template and Document Files

There are four primary types of files used in Word:

- A *document file* (.doc) is created and named whenever a new document is saved. Documents contain text, formatting information, styles, macros, fonts, embedded graphics, and customizations to the Word interface. Word can also open other types of document files—such as rich-text files (.rtf) or text files (.txt)—but these do not have all the functionality of a Word document.

- A *template file* (.dot) contains all the same elements as a document, and can also hold formatted AutoText entries (see Part 2 for more on AutoText). Template files are used to hold collections of styles, customizations, and boilerplate text and to associate those collections with documents. Every document has at least one template attached to it. When you create a new document, it is always based on a template. New blank documents are based on *Normal.dot*, but you can base a document on any template. You can also attach a template to an existing document to make its collection of styles and so on available to the document (use Tools → Templates and

---

Add-Ins → Attach). Only one template may be attached to a document at a time.

NOTE

From Windows Explorer, right-click a template (.dot) file and select New to create a new document with that template attached. Find out more about using templates in Part 2.

- A *temporary file* (.tmp) is created when an existing document is opened or a new document is saved for the first time. Word uses this file (and may create additional .tmp files) to track changes while a document is open. The files are stored in the same directory as the document and are discarded when the document is closed. These files are hidden in Windows Explorer and have the same name as the main document file, except that the first letter of the filename is replaced by a tilde (~) and the second by a dollar sign. Unfortunately, these files are used only as "working space" by Word and you cannot really recover any meaningful information from them when Word crashes.

NOTE

Word often leaves .tmp files lying around (after a crash, for example). Word uses temporary files to determine the state of a document, so if a document won't open or save, look in the document's folder for a leftover .tmp file and delete it.

- If Word's AutoRecover feature is enabled (Tools → Options → Save → Save AutoRecover info every *x* Minutes) an AutoRecover file is created when a document is opened and is updated at a specified interval. In the event of a crash, you can usually recover the most recent update just by restarting Word. You can find a list of locations where AutoRecover files are stored (and other common file locations) in Part 3.

How Templates Are Loaded

The Word interface—the menus and toolbars, commands, available styles, keyboard shortcuts, and so on—are all loaded into Word in layers each time you start the program. The complete interface that you see is called the *global layer* and is built in the following manner:

1. When you start Word, the program files begin to build the framework for the interface. Menus and toolbars are loaded programmatically.

2. Word loads a global template named *Normal.dot*, which contains styles and any customizations that you have made to the Word interface—custom menus, keyboard shortcuts, and so on. These customizations override the interface elements loaded in step 1.

3. Word loads any template files (those ending in .dot) that are located in various startup and template folders. These locations are listed in Part 3. Each of the templates loaded may contain customizations or features that override or add to the interface features loaded in steps 1 and 2.

4. At this point, Word's global layer is built, but not necessarily finalized. You can manually load additional templates using Tools → Templates and Add-Ins → Add. The Templates and Add-Ins dialog box shows all currently loaded templates and lets you remove templates. You can also create or load documents at this point, which in turn may load additional templates.

It is important to understand this basic procedure for a number of reasons. Any customizations you perform on the Word interface or macros or styles that you create must be saved in a template. If you save them in *Normal.dot* (the default choice most of the time), they are available to all documents. If you save them in a particular template, they are available to documents only when those templates are loaded. Understanding this procedure and being able to selectively load templates also helps you troubleshoot when things don't work as predicted. For example, a style that you customized and saved in *Normal.dot* may not be formatted the way you intend if another template loads another version of the style.

NOTE

Launch Word from the command line using the /a switch (word.exe /a) to start up without loading *Normal.dot*, templates in the Startup folder, add-in libraries, or user settings stored in the Registry. See Part 3 for details on other switches and how to use them.

Tips on Using Templates

The following are some tips for working with templates and documents in Word. You'll find advice on performing other template-related tasks in Part 2.

- *Normal.dot* is the king of templates, and is always loaded when Word starts—you don't get a choice. All customizations, styles, macros, and so on are saved in *Normal. dot*, unless you specify another template. AutoCorrect entries that have any formatting in them are stored in *Normal.dot*, as are all AutoText entries. You can copy *Normal.dot* to other computers to carry your settings with you. The table of common file locations in Part 3 shows where *Normal.dot* is stored on different kinds of systems.

- Any customizations, styles, etc. applied to the current document override those found in the current template, which in turn override settings found in *Normal.dot*, which in turn override those found in the application itself. For example, you could assign the Ctrl-Shift-D key combination to the Paste Special command. Saving that customization in *Normal.dot* makes the key combination work in any open document. Saving it in another template makes it work in any document the template was attached to (or whenever the template was loaded as an add-in). Saving the key combination in a document makes it work only in that document.

- The shortcut menu of a Word document in Windows Explorer (the menu you get when you right-click on a file in a folder window) has commands for opening the file, printing it using the default printer settings in Word, and viewing the file's properties—which include the name, type, location, and size, as well as the dates that the file was created, last modified, and last accessed. Template files have the same commands on their shortcut menu and also feature a command for creating a new document based on the template.

- You'll see several kinds of templates mentioned in Word documentation, including global, user, and workgroup templates. However, all templates are really the same; the only thing that differs is their use. Global templates are added when word loads (through Tools → Templates and Add-Ins). User templates are stored on a user's computer and are typically attached when creating a new document. Workgroup templates are loaded in the same way as user templates, but are often stored on a network server and intended for use by all members of a workgroup. Since templates can contain text (just like documents), you can use them to create boilerplates. For example, you could create a template of a letter with text that you use regularly, and format that text appropriately. When you create a new document from the template, the boilerplate text appears and you can just "fill in the blanks."

- The various documents you can create by selecting File → New are based on templates. When you save a template, the default save location is the main Templates folder used by Word (check out Part 3 for details on common file locations). Templates saved in this folder are available for creating new documents when you select File → New → General Templates → General.

- When a template is attached to a document (either when a document is created based on the template or a new template is attached later), all of the styles, macros, and other goodies are copied to the document file. Items in the document that are not in the template are unaffected. Items in the document with identical names to items in the template are replaced. If the items in the template are updated later, the Tools → Templates and Add-Ins → Automatically update document styles setting determines whether the same items in the document are updated automatically or not.

How a Document Works

Every Word document is made up of three layers—a main text layer sandwiched between front and back drawing layers (Figure 4). The main text layer contains the text of a document, and can also hold two types of objects:

- *Inline objects* appear in line with the text in the main text layer and behave as though they were a single character. The insertion point moves over an inline object just like it moves over a character. Text does not wrap around inline objects. With the exception of text boxes and drawing objects (WordArt, Charts, etc.), all objects are inserted as inline objects by default.

NOTE

Inline objects are best used when the object should behave as a character, since inline objects can be moved and formatted in the same way as characters. For example, you might want to format the object using tabs, indents, and paragraph or character formatting.

- *Framed objects* have a frame around them (which may or may not be visible) that affects the way text flows around

---

the object. Framed objects are really a holdover from previous versions of Word that did not have drawing layers. Floating objects, which are discussed next, have rendered framed objects obsolete.

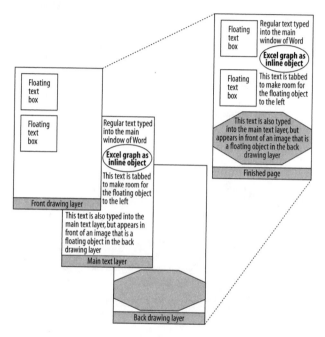

Figure 4. The layers of a document (with text callouts)

The front and back drawing layers of a document are like transparencies laid on top of and under the text layer of a document. Only floating objects, such as drawings or text boxes, exist in these layers. Floating objects can be stacked on top of one another within a layer. For example, suppose there are two objects in the back drawing layer (behind the text): one a background graphic for a newsletter and the other a text box with an advertisement. Those two objects could be stacked so that the graphic appeared behind the textbox, creating an additional layering effect even though both objects are on the same drawing layer (Figure 5).

NOTE

Three additional layers that work identically to the three main layers are used to create headers and footers in a document. These additional layers (known as the header/footer layers) are all positioned behind the main back drawing layer. This means that any objects or text in the main drawing or text layers will always obscure objects and text in the header/footer layers.

Figure 5. Stacking floating objects within a layer

Floating objects can be either anchored to a particular paragraph or unanchored. An object anchored to a paragraph moves when the paragraph moves. An unanchored object stays where it is on the page, unaffected when you move text.

You can choose whether text should wrap around a floating object (as it would with a framed object) or whether it should be shown on top of or beneath the text (depending on which drawing layer it's in). To do this, select the object and use Format → Object → Layout. The command *Object* in your Format menu may vary, depending on the actual type of object (i.e., Picture, AutoShape, etc.) that is selected.

In Word 2002, floating objects are automatically inserted onto a drawing "canvas" that basically works to group the objects so that they can be moved together and can share a common border and background. The canvas is represented by a separate frame around the object. You can remove objects from this canvas by dragging them and you can delete the canvas itself by selecting it and pressing Delete. To prevent Word from creating the canvas, use Tools → Options → General → Automatically create drawing canvas when inserting AutoShapes.

Formatting

Regardless of how you think your document is constructed (words form sentences, which form paragraphs, which form pages, etc.), Word sees all documents as having three parts:

- A document has one or more *sections*.
- A section has zero or more *paragraphs*.
- A paragraph has one or more *characters*.

Word also has three types of formatting: section, paragraph, and character—one for each of the three parts. While Word's interface often makes it seem like formatting can be applied to an entire document or to specific pages, formatting is really just being applied to sections of the document.

Sections

Sections are used to control the flow of a document (by forcing page and column breaks) and to set up page formatting. All new documents start life with one section that contains everything you type. That changes when one of the following happens:

- You insert a section break manually using Insert → Break and choosing one of the section break types. A Next page break inserts a section break and starts a new section on the next page. A Continuous break inserts a section, but does not start a new page. An Odd or Even page break inserts a section break and starts a new section on the next odd or even page.

- You change formatting on a range of pages, a single page, or even part of a page in the document. Remember, Word doesn't really see pages—just sections. To change formatting for part of a document, a section must be created that holds that part. Such formatting includes changing the orientation, margins, or page layout for a page (or range of pages) or setting up page numbering.

NOTE

Section breaks are visible by default only in Word's Normal view, where they appear as dashed horizontal lines labeled according to the type of break. You can force section breaks to appear in other views using Tools → Options → View → Hidden, but they are not as easy to see or use as in Normal view.

Paragraphs

The paragraph is the most important element in a Word document. The ultimate success of every bit of formatting in a document depends on the paragraph. In Word, a paragraph is a paragraph mark (¶) plus all of the text preceding that paragraph mark up to, but not including, the previous paragraph mark or the beginning of the document (Figure 6).

From Walden¶

¶

I also heard the whooping of the ice in the pond, my great bed-fellow in that part of Concord, as if it were restless in its bed and would fain turn over, were troubled with flatulency and had dreams; or I was waked by the cracking of the ground by the frost, as if some one had driven a team against my door, and in the morning would find a crack in the earth a quarter of a mile long and a third of an inch wide. ¶

Sometimes I heard the foxes as they ranged over the snow-crust, in moonlight nights, in search of a partridge or other game, barking raggedly and demoniacally like forest dogs, as if laboring with some anxiety, or seeking expression, struggling for light and to be dogs outright and run freely in the streets; for if we take the ages into our account, may there not be a civilization going on among brutes as well as men? They seemed to me to be rudimental, burrowing men, still standing on their defence, awaiting their transformation. Sometimes one came near to my window, attracted by my light, barked a vulpine curse at me, and then retreated. ¶

¶

Figure 6. Selecting a whole paragraph, including the paragraph mark

---

NOTE

To create a well-formatted document, you must be able to see Word's paragraph marks. You can force Word to show them using the Show/Hide button on the Standard toolbar. However, this also turns on a lot of other hidden characters (like spaces and tabs) that many people find distracting. Instead, use Tools → Options → View → Formatting to turn on just the formatting characters you want to see. Even if you only turn on paragraph marks, your life in Word is about to become a lot better.

The paragraph mark

The paragraph mark is a character that has a font, size, and color, and just like other characters, you can move, copy, and even delete paragraph marks. However, the paragraph mark also contains all of the formatting information for a paragraph (both character and paragraph formatting). The number of paragraph marks in a document is equal to the number of paragraphs. Every time you press the Enter key, a new paragraph is created and a new paragraph mark is placed in the document.

Following are some of the things that make a paragraph mark so special:

- It holds all the formatting information for that paragraph, including character formatting—fonts, sizes, style, color, indents, outline level, bullets, and any tabs that were pressed in the paragraph as well as any tab settings put into effect within the scope of the paragraph. Unless overridden by applying manual character formatting (Format → Font), every character in the paragraph takes on the formatting applied to the paragraph mark.

NOTE

While paragraph formatting is contained in the paragraph mark, you cannot adjust a paragraph's format by selecting the mark and applying new formats directly to it. This action just applies character formatting to the paragraph mark itself.

- It is the end of a paragraph. No text may be typed after the paragraph mark. Using the right arrow to move over it causes the insertion point to move to the beginning of the next paragraph. The End key jumps to the end of any line, but if that line contains a paragraph mark, it jumps to a position right in front of the mark.
- It always ends a document. The final character in a document is always the paragraph mark. Word associates a wide variety of formatting with the final paragraph mark, especially section and style formatting.

Tips on using paragraphs

Following are some tips on using paragraphs and paragraph marks in Word.

- When you are typing a paragraph and hit Enter, a new paragraph mark (and thus a new paragraph) is created. The formatting style applied to the new paragraph is defined by the Format → Style → *any style* → Modify → "Style for following paragraph" option. By default, unless a different style is specified here, the new paragraph uses the same style as the previous paragraph. Styles are covered later in this part.

- You can select a paragraph in two ways: by clicking and dragging to select all the text in the paragraph (or in multiple paragraphs) or by triple-clicking anywhere in the paragraph. If paragraph marks are visible in your document (and they always should be), you can make sure the entire paragraph and formatting are selected by making sure the paragraph mark is selected. Once selected, you can move or copy the paragraph to a new location and keep its formatting intact.

- You can select all of the text in a paragraph and not the paragraph mark itself by clicking to the left of the paragraph mark and then clicking at the beginning of the paragraph while holding the Alt key. You can then move or copy the text to another location without carrying over the formatting or creating a new paragraph in the new location (i.e., you could paste into an existing paragraph).

Characters

Characters are the smallest pieces of a document. This is a significant fact to bear in mind when selecting and formatting text. A single character in a word, a single word (a collection of characters) in a paragraph, or even a blank space can be formatted simply by selecting the text and applying a different format to it.

To Word, every non-navigational key pressed inserts a character. Some characters appear as printable text, others as non-printing characters. Tabs, returns, spaces, page breaks, and section breaks are all characters in a document. Select, move, or delete them just like any other character. This very fact explains a lot of the strange things that go on in Word. Use the Show/Hide tool to display these non-printing characters in a document (Figure 7).

Figure 7. Paragraph marks, tabs, and space characters appearing in Show/Hide mode

Styles

A style is a collection of formatting information that has been given a name. Applying a style applies all the formatting in that style at once. There are two types of styles in Word:

- *Paragraph styles* contain formatting that is applied to an entire paragraph. Paragraph styles can include paragraph formatting (such as tabs, line spacing, and indenting), character formatting (such as font, size, and color), and formatting that applies to either characters or paragraphs (such as borders or languages).

- *Character styles* contain formatting that is applied only to selected characters within a paragraph. Characters within a paragraph can have their own style even if a different character style is applied to the paragraph as a whole. Character styles can only include character formatting.

Apply either type of style by selecting it from the Style drop-down list on the Standard toolbar. Paragraph styles are noted with a paragraph mark (¶) and character styles are noted with an underlined letter *a*. Paragraph styles are applied to the paragraph that contains the insertion point or to multiple selected paragraphs. Character styles are applied to selected text.

TIP

The Style box on the Standard toolbar displays the current paragraph's style, unless the current selection has a character style applied, in which case you'll see only the character style in the Style box. The paragraph style is still there, but the character style is the one that shows up in the box. To see both the character and paragraph styles for a selection, use Format → Reveal Formatting.

Character styles override paragraph styles. Applying a paragraph style to an existing paragraph changes all of the paragraph formatting to that specified in the style. This includes line spacing, tabs, indents, etc. It also changes the format of all of the characters in the paragraph to match that specified in the style, *except* for characters that have formatting applied directly to them. For example, suppose you have a paragraph formatted in the Normal style and you add special formatting to one word in the paragraph (say, italicize it and make the font red for emphasis) by either applying the changes directly or using a character style. If you then apply a new paragraph style that uses a different font, all the characters in the paragraph would change except for that word.

NOTE

Quickly remove all character formatting by selecting a range of characters and pressing Ctrl-Spacebar. This causes the characters to revert to the character formatting defined in the paragraph style. Remove manual paragraph formatting from a paragraph by selecting the whole paragraph, including the paragraph mark, and pressing Ctrl-Q.

Shortcut Menus

If you have used Windows for any amount of time, you are likely familiar with shortcut menus—the contextual menus of commands you get when you right-click an item. Right-clicking also works in Word and is a real time-saver. Generally, right-clicking an element inside the document window (text, graphics, etc.) provides access to the same commands you would find on the regular menus for dealing with that element.

Following is a summary of what right-clicking gets you in the Word interface:

- Whether you right-click a selected word, paragraph, or just somewhere within text, you get a shortcut menu with editing commands (copy, cut, paste), formatting commands (font, paragraph, bullets, and numbering), some language tools, and a command for selecting all paragraphs in the document that use the same style as the selected paragraph.

- If the text has special attributes (maybe it's underlined as a misspelled word, a revision using Word's Track Changes feature, indented, or a bulleted list), you also get commands for dealing with that function (e.g., spelling corrections).

- An object's shortcut menu provides commands for grouping, ordering, and formatting the object.

- Right-clicking a table (or a selected part of a table) provides most of the commands found on the Table menu.

- The shortcut menu of any command bar displays a list of common command bars you can toggle on or off.

- Right-clicking the TRK button on the status bar lets you turn Track Changes on and set options.

- Right-clicking the Spelling and Grammar status button on the status bar lets you hide or show spelling and grammar errors and set options.

Unique to the Word interface is the ability to customize the commands that appear on the shortcut menus, just as you can customize commands on the command bars. First, select Tools → Customize → Toolbars → Shortcut Menus. This opens a special command bar named Shortcut Menus that stays open only until you close the Customize dialog. The three menus on this command bar hold submenus that correspond to all shortcut menus available in Word. For example, the Text → Text menu is the shortcut menu for basic text. While this command bar is open, you can use the commands found on the Commands tab of the Customize dialog to drag any of the commands available in Word to any shortcut menu (or to any menu or toolbar, for that matter). For example, you might want to add the ApplyHeading1, 2, and 3 commands to the Text → Text shortcut menu so that you can apply headings just by right-clicking.

What Word Tries to Do for You

Word performs many behind-the-scenes actions that some people can't do without and some people can't stand. You've already learned about AutoRecover, which saves files in the background every few minutes in case Word crashes (this is a good feature). The other three big automated features are AutoCorrect, "smart" cut and paste, and background spelling and grammar checking.

AutoCorrect

When you start typing a list using asterisks as bullets, Word converts it to a bulleted list. When you accidentally type "teh", Word changes it to "the" as soon as you hit the spacebar. These, and many others, are part of Word's AutoCorrect feature, which is essentially a long list of suspect things that Word should watch for and the text or formatting it should use to replace those things when it detects them.

You can also control the corrections you want Word to apply. Just go to Tools → AutoCorrect Options. The two important tabs on this dialog for dealing with automatic options are:

AutoCorrect

This tab controls actual text corrections. The options at the top of the dialog deal mostly with incorrect capitalization. The "Replace text as you type" option specifies whether the long list of corrections at the bottom of the dialog should be used. The left column is what should be replaced; the right column is what replaces it. You can delete items from the list or add your own items by entering them in the topmost fields.

AutoFormat As You Type

These options control automatic formatting—bulleted and numbered lists, smart quotes (the curly quotes), and fraction characters, to name a few.

Smart Cut and Paste

Smart Cut and Paste is the feature that automatically controls spacing as you paste text into a location. For the most part, this feature is benign. It is helpful to copy a group of words, paste them into a new paragraph, and have Word make one space at the beginning and end of the group. Depending on your tastes, though, you may want to fine tune the Smart Cut and Paste settings.

First, go to Tools → Options → Edit. The Smart Cut and Paste option turns the whole feature on and off. If it's turned on, use the Settings button to control individual pasting options. Some of the more interesting options include:

- Merging pasted lists with the surrounding list in the destination location
- Adjusting table alignment when pasting tables or parts of tables into new locations
- Adjusting sentence, word, and paragraph spacing when pasting

Spelling and Grammar

By default, Word checks both spelling and grammar in the background while you're working on a document. Word puts squiggly red lines under words that don't match its dictionary and squiggly green lines under suspected grammatical errors. You can right-click the errors and see suggested corrections on the shortcut menu. While it sounds useful, most people find it distracting and resource-consuming. Go to Tools → Options → Spelling and Grammar to control it. If you want Word to do the background checking but not show the errors in the document, select the hide options in both the Spelling and Grammar sections. To turn background checking off altogether, clear the "Check spelling" and "Check grammar as you type" options. The rest of the options deal with how Word checks spelling and grammar, and are covered more in Part 2.

PART II

Word Tasks

This main section of the book is designed to give you quick answers about how to perform tasks in Word; we hope it will introduce you to many tasks you might not yet know about. Tasks are divided into the following sixteen categories:

- Working with Files
- Printing
- Moving Around in a Document
- Entering and Editing Text
- Formatting
- Changing Your View
- Controlling the Flow of a Document
- Inserting Fields and Reference Items
- Inserting Objects
- Working with Tables
- Spelling and Other Tools
- Setting Other Word Options
- Getting Help
- Customizing Word
- Collaborating
- Using Macros

Within these categories, tasks are presented as answers to "How do I..." questions (e.g., "How do I print pages in reverse order?"), followed by concise instructions for completing the task. For some task questions, there are multiple solutions.

Working with Files

Use the following answers to help you create, find, save, and
work with files.

How do I...

Create a new Word document without starting Word?
Right-click any blank space in a folder or desktop and
select New → Microsoft Word Document.

Create a new document within Word?
New Blank Document button on Standard toolbar or
Ctrl-N creates a new blank document based on the *Nor-
mal.dot* template.

File → New; create a blank document of any type, base
the new document on an existing document.

Create a document from a template?
In Word 2002, use File → New → General Templates. In
Word 97 and 2000, use File → New. Select a template
from the Templates dialog.

Open a document?
File → Open, Ctrl-O, or the Open button to bring up the
Open dialog; browse for an existing document. Use the
Open drop-down list on the dialog to open in different
ways (read-only, open a copy, etc.).

Find a Document?
In Word 2002, File → Search; enter the text, location,
and file types to search for documents with specific text

in them. Click Advanced Search to search using multiple criteria in one step.

In Word 97 and 2000, use the Find command on the Tools menu of the File → Open dialog box.

Save a document?

File → Save, Save button, or Ctrl-S to save recent work on a document.

File → Save As to save using a different name or in a different location. File → Save opens the Save As dialog the first time you save a document.

File → Save as Web Page (Save as HTML in Word 97) to convert a document to HTML.

Close all open documents with one command?

Hold down Shift key while opening the File menu to change the Close command to Close All.

Tools → Customize → Commands to add Close All button to a toolbar. See "Customizing Word" later in this part.

Add my own templates to the Templates dialog box?

Create a template and then save it in *C:\Documents and Settings\<username>\Application Data\Microsoft\ Templates* (for Windows 2000/XP) or in *C:\ Windows\Application Data\Microsoft\Templates* (for Windows 9x/Me). In Word 97 (on any Windows), save it in *C:\Program Files\Microsoft Office\Templates*. Create a new subfolder in the Templates folder to create a new tab on the Templates dialog.

Keep track of different versions of documents?

File → Versions → Save Now to save recent work as a new version and enter comments. Saved versions are listed by date and time.

Change the summary information for a document?

File → Properties → Summary; enter information about the document.

Save a preview picture with a template?
> File → Properties → Summary → Save preview picture.

Set up custom properties for a document?
> File → Properties → Custom; select properties from the list to add to the document.

Change how many recently used files are shown on the File menu?
> Tools → Options → General; turn the option on or off and select from 1–9 recent files to appear.

Copy a backup of the previous version of a document whenever I save?
> Tools → Options → Save → Always create backup copy. Word saves the previous version in the same folder with a .wbk extension.

Change the default format used to save documents?
> Tools → Options → Save; use the "Save Word files as" drop-down list to choose a format.

Make sure others have the fonts used in my document?

 Tools → Options → Save → Embed TrueType fonts. You can also embed only the characters in use (and for Word 2000 and 2002 skip the common system fonts), since font embedding increases file size.

Control the default locations where files and templates are saved?
> Tools → Options → File Locations. See Part 3 for a list of default file locations.

2+ *Keep personal information from being saved with a document?*
> Tools → Options → Security → Remove personal information from this File on save.

2+ *Recover a document after Word crashes?*
> Start Word. The Document Recovery task pane opens automatically, listing files that were recovered. You can compare the recovered files to the previously saved versions and decide which to keep.

Change how often AutoRecover information is saved?
Tools → Options → Save → Save AutoRecover information every *xx* minutes.

Change where AutoRecover information is saved?
Tools → Options → File Locations → AutoRecover Files → Modify.

Recover the text without formatting from any document?

Make sure the Tools → Options → General → "Confirm conversion at open" option is enabled. Select File → Open, find the file, then select the Recover Text From Any File option in the File of Type dropdown list.

02+ *Recover Word when the program hangs?*
Start → All Programs → Microsoft Office Tools → Microsoft Office Application Recovery. This dialog lets you end a frozen program (losing all document changes) or attempt to recover the program and any documents.

02+ *Start Word in safe mode when it won't start normally?*
Hold down Ctrl when you start Word or type word.exe /safe at the command prompt. Some restrictions apply in safe mode. Templates cannot be saved, the Office Assistant is not loaded, customizations are not loaded, recovered documents are not opened, preferences cannot be saved, and the AutoCorrect list is not loaded.

02+ *Enable items that are disabled in safe mode?*
Help → About Microsoft Word → Disabled Items; select the items you want to enable and click Enable.

Printing

The following tasks show you various ways to print, how to set up a page and control printer options, and how to use the Print Preview feature.

How do I...

Print a document?
> File → Print or Ctrl-P; select printer, options, and click Print.

Print a document from Windows?
> Right-click the document (or group of selected documents) and select Print. Word opens long enough to print the document using default settings and then closes.

Print one copy of a document without using the Print dialog?
> Print button on Standard toolbar prints one copy using default settings.

Print to a file instead of a printer?
> File → Print → Print to File.

Print using draft output to save time and ink?
> File → Print → Options → Print using draft output.
>
> Tools → Options → Print → Print using draft output.

Choose what information is printed along with a document?
> File → Print → Options (or Tools → Options → Print); use the options in the Include with Document section of the dialog.

Set other printing options?
> File → Print → Options or Tools → Options → Print.

Change the margins for a section or an entire document?
> File → Page Setup → Margins; use the boxes in the Margins section of the dialog. A gutter is extra space added to the margin for binding.

Change page orientation for a section or document?
> In Word 2000 and 2002, File → Page Setup → Margins → Orientation; choose portrait or landscape.
>
> In Word 97, File → Page Setup → Paper Size → Orientation.

00+ *Change how multiple pages are printed?*

File → Print → Pages per sheet; print up to sixteen pages on one sheet of paper.

File → Page Setup → Margins → Multiple Pages; mirror margins creates facing-page layouts (where left and right pages face one another), 2 pages per sheet prints two identical pages on each sheet of paper, book fold puts two different pages on a single sheet and is designed for documents (like invitations) that fold in the middle.

Configure settings for paper size, type, and source?

File → Page Setup → Paper. Word 97 has separate Paper Size and Paper Source tabs.

Change how headers and footers are printed?

File → Page Setup → Page Layout; use options in Headers and Footers section of dialog.

Change the vertical alignment of pages in a section or document?

File → Page Setup → Page Layout → Vertical Alignment.

Print pages in reverse order (last to first)?

File → Print → Options (or Tools → Options → Print); select Reverse print order. If you print a document in reverse order that is also set to print more than one page per sheet, the order of all the pages is reversed *before* putting them on the sheets, which is probably not the result you'd want.

02+ *Print two-sided pages without add-on software?*

If you have a duplex printer (one that can print both sides of paper at once), set options using File → Print → Options (or Tools → Options → Print). Options controlling how Word prints each side are at the bottom of the dialog.

If you don't have a duplex printer, select File → Print → Manual Duplex. After one side prints, Word prompts you to reinsert the paper to print on the other side.

Print information in a document other than text?

File → Print → Print What; print document properties, markup, styles, AutoText entries, and shortcut keys.

Preview a document before printing?

File → Print Preview. You can zoom and view multiple pages at once. Make sure you use the Close button on the toolbar to return to the regular document view.

Moving Around in a Document

The following solutions show you how to move the insertion point and the display view of a document. This section also shows you how to find and replace text, and how to browse for specific objects.

How do I...

Scroll around in a document?

Click the arrows at the edge of the vertical scroll bar to move up and down one line at a time. Click the area above or below the scroll handle to move up or down one page. Drag the scroll handle to move the view freely; a pop-up balloon shows the page and major headings as you scroll past. Scrolling using the scroll bars changes your view, but does *not* move the insertion point. Use the horizontal scroll bar much as you would the vertical scroll bar.

TIP

Hold the Shift key while clicking the left scroll arrow to scroll left beyond the margin.

Hide the scroll bars?

Tools → Options → View; use the Horizontal and Vertical Scroll bar options.

Move the insertion point with the keyboard?

Left and Right arrows to move one character at a time. Add Ctrl key to move words instead of characters. Add Shift key to select text while moving.

Up and down arrows to move one line at a time. Add Ctrl key to move paragraphs instead of lines. Add Shift key to select text while moving.

See a complete list of movement keys in Part 3.

See where the screen view is in the document?

The leftmost number on the status bar (Page *x*) displays the number of the page you are viewing (Figure 8). You can also click and hold the vertical scroll handle to see the page and nearest heading.

Figure 8. View and insertion point location

See where the insertion point is in the document?

The second and third values on the status bar (Sec *x* and *y/yy*) show the section and page where the insertion point is located. Also on the status bar, "At" shows distance from the top margin of the current page, "Ln" shows the line number, and "Col" shows the column number.

Center the view on the insertion point?

Click any movement key (such as the right arrow) to center the view.

Go to a specific location in a document?

Edit → Go To or Ctrl-G; select the object (page, table, graphic, etc.) and click Next or Previous to browse objects of that type. Enter a specific value (e.g., page number, bookmark name) to go directly to it.

Return to where I left off the last time I had the document open?

Shift-F5 when you first open the document. Shift-F5 also moves you to the last three places you made changes if the document has been open.

Find specific text in a document?

Edit → Find or Ctrl-F; type the text and click Find Next.

Find and select all occurrences of specific text in a document?

Edit → Find; type the text, select the Highlight all items option, and click Find All. All occurrences are selected. Typing or deleting affects only the first occurrence. Using Edit → Copy copies all occurrences to the clipboard.

Find specific formatting in a document?

Edit → Find → More → Format; choose an option and use the resulting dialog to specify formatting to search for. Each selection adds a format to the search criteria. You can search for text and multiple formats (e.g., occurrences of a particular word that are also bold and italicized) simultaneously. Click No Formatting to remove all formatting from the search.

Find special characters in a document?

Edit → Find → More → Special; choose the character from the list. See Part 3 for a list of search codes you can use when searching.

Find and replace text in a document?

Edit → Replace or Ctrl-H; type the text to find, the text to replace it with, and click Find Next to select the next occurrence in the document. Click Replace to replace the current selection or Replace All to replace all found occurrences.

Find and replace specific formatting?

Edit → Replace → More → Format.

Find and replace special characters?
   Edit → Replace → More → Special.

Find or replace noun or adjective forms or verb tenses?
   Edit → Find or Edit → Replace; click More and select Find all word forms.

Browse a document by specific objects?
   Click the Select Browse Object button (under the vertical scroll bar) or press Ctrl-Alt-Home; select the type of object to browse from the pop-up menu. Click the Previous and Next buttons (or Ctrl-Page Up and Ctrl-Page Down) to do the browsing.

TIP

There is no way to assign a custom keyboard shortcut directly to the Find Next command (although Alt-F works with the dialog box open). If you want to close the Find dialog box and still do a Find Next, do the first search, close the dialog box, and then use Ctrl-Page Down to find subsequent occurrences.

Entering and Editing Text

The following solutions show you ways to enter new text, and also how to select and manipulate existing text.

Using AutoText and AutoCorrect

How do I...

Create an AutoText entry for inserting frequently used text and graphics?
   In the document window, type and then select the text you want to use. Choose Insert → AutoText → AutoText. Click Add to create the entry. Optionally, you can type a different name for the entry before clicking Add.

Insert an AutoText entry?

Insert → Autotext; select an AutoText entry from one of the submenus. You can also type the first few letters of the entry and press F3. If Tools → Options → View → Screen Tips is enabled, a pop-up balloon with the Auto-Text entry also appears after the first few letters are typed; press Enter to accept the suggestion and insert the AutoText.

TIP

Right-click anywhere on the toolbar area and select Auto-Text to show a toolbar with all the AutoText entries.

Turn off the pop-up AutoComplete suggestions for AutoText entries?

Tools → Options → View → Screen Tips. This also turns off other screen tips, such as those that show the names of toolbar buttons.

Undo an AutoCorrect insertion?

AutoCorrect entries (like replacing "(c)" with the copyright symbol) are inserted automatically as you type. As soon as it happens, choose Edit → Undo or Ctrl-Z to undo the autocorrection.

Control AutoCorrect options?

Tools → AutoCorrect Options → AutoCorrect.

Inserting Text and Other Elements

How do I...

Insert the current date and time into a document?

Insert → Date and Time; select the Update Automatically option to have Word always display the current date and time in the document.

Insert a symbol?

Insert → Symbol → Symbols. Choose a font and subset, select the symbol, and click Insert. For frequently used symbols, click Shortcut Key to assign a keyboard short-cut.

Insert a special character?
Insert → Symbol → Special Characters.

Keep text from disappearing as I type?
If new characters that you type replace existing characters (instead of just bumping them to the right to make room for the new text), the Overtype feature is turned on. The OVR on the status bar is active when Overtype is enabled. Turn it off by pressing Insert, double-clicking the word OVR on the status bar, or by using Tools → Options → Edit → Overtype mode.

Selecting Text

How do I...

Select a character?
Click and drag over that character. To select the character immediately left or right of the insertion point, hold Shift and click the left or right arrow key. Keep pressing the arrow keys to extend the selection one character at a time in that direction.

Select a word?
Double-click the word. Use Ctrl-Shift-Left (or Right) to select the word immediately to the left or right. Keep pressing the arrow keys to extend the selection one word at a time.

Select a sentence?
Click and Drag over that sentence.

TIP

The SentLeftExtend and SentRightExtend commands extend the selection one sentence to the left or right (much like Shift-Left or Right extends by characters). Put them on a toolbar or assign shortcut keys to them.

Select a paragraph?

Triple-click the paragraph. Use Ctrl-Shift-Up or Down to extend a selection from the insertion point to the beginning or end of the paragraph. Keep pressing the up or down arrow to extend the selection one paragraph at a time.

Select a specific group of characters?

Click one location and then Shift-click another location to select all full words between the two locations. Use Alt instead of Shift to select specific characters instead of full words.

02+ *Select multiple non-contiguous pieces of text?*

Make the first selection using any method (e.g., double-click to select a word). Hold the Ctrl key down while making another selection elsewhere in the document. Keep holding the Ctrl key down to add more selections.

02+

> **Select all paragraphs using a particular style or format?**
>
> Make a selection or place the insertion point in the appropriate location, then choose Format → Styles and Formatting → Select All.
>
> Right-click a selection or location and choose Select Text With Similar Formatting from the shortcut menu.

02+ *Change whether the paragraph mark is selected along with a paragraph?*

Tools → Options → Edit → Use smart paragraph selection. Selecting the paragraph mark moves formatting with the paragraph and does not leave behind an empty paragraph. This option applies only when selecting the paragraph by dragging over the text. Triple-clicking always selects the paragraph mark.

Change whether whole words are automatically selected when I drag over them?

Tools → Options → Edit; enable or disable the "When selecting, automatically select entire word" option.

Use the Extend Selection (EXT) feature?

Press F8 or double-click EXT on the status bar to enter the Extend Selection mode. In this mode, take one of the following actions:

- Click anywhere to extend the selection from the insertion point.

- Use the arrow keys to extend the selection one line (up and down arrows) or one character (left and right arrows) at a time.

- Press F8 repeatedly to extend the selection. The first press after entering the mode selects the word closest to the insertion point. The second click selects the entire sentence, third the entire paragraph, fourth the whole document.

- Press Esc to exit EXT mode.

Copying and Pasting

How do I...

Move or copy text by dragging?

Select the text using any method and then click and drag the text to a new location. You can drag somewhere else in the same document, to another open document, or to a document in another program that supports it (such as Excel or Outlook).

TIP

Drag a selection to the Windows Desktop to create a *document scrap*—a special file with an .shs extension. You cannot open this file, but you can drag it into any open document to insert the text there with formatting.

02+ *Get rid of the paste options button that appears over text when I paste?*

Tools → Options → Edit → Show Paste Options button.

00+ *Copy multiple items to the Office Clipboard?*

The Office Clipboard lets you collect (by copying or cutting) up to 24 items from any Office document (12 items in Word 2000). Open the clipboard using Edit → Office Clipboard. Copy items using standard copy and cut commands.

Click Paste All to items to the current location; click Clear All to clear the clipboard.

02+ *Change whether the Office Clipboard appears when I copy multiple items?*

Edit → Office Clipboard → Options. The Show Office Clipboard automatically option causes the clipboard to appear when you copy two items consecutively. The Collect Without Showing Office Clipboard option lets you collect items without the task pane showing.

Paste items using alternate or special formatting?

Edit → Paste Special; choose a format and click OK.

Formatting

The following solutions show you how to apply character and paragraph formatting, and also how to use and organize formatting styles.

Character Formatting

How do I...

Apply basic font formatting?

Format → Font; set font, style, size, and color for new text typed at the insertion point or to change the format of selected text. You can also access these controls on the Formatting toolbar.

Apply special font effects?

Format → Font; use any of the options in the Effects section.

Hide text?

Select text, then use Format → Font → Hidden. Use the Show/Hide button or Tools → Options → View → Hidden Text to see hidden text.

Use a drop cap in a paragraph?

Format → Drop Cap; place the drop cap within the text or in the margin. You can also select a font for the capitalized letter, specify how many lines to drop (1–3), and change the distance from the other letters.

Set a default font?

Format → Font; select the font and its attributes, and then click Default. Changes are saved in *Normal.dot*.

Use or remove text animations?

Format → Font → Text Effects (Format → Font → Animation in Word 97).

Turn on or off text animations without removing them from a document?

Tools → Options → View → Animated Text.

Change the spacing between characters?

Format → Font → Character Spacing. Scale stretches or condenses text horizontally. Spacing increases or reduces the space between characters. Position changes the position of the text vertically in relation to the baseline. Kerning changes the spacing between certain predefined letter combinations so that words look more evenly spaced; you can control the font size at which kerning occurs.

Paragraph Formatting

How do I...

Change the alignment of a paragraph?

Place the insertion point in or select the paragraph. Then use the Align Left, Center, Align Right, and Justify

buttons on the Formatting toolbar or go to Format →
Paragraph → Indents and Spacing → Alignment.

Change the indentation of a paragraph?

Place the insertion point at the beginning of a paragraph
or select multiple paragraphs, then take one of the following actions:

- Set the left indent by dragging the Left Indent marker
  (the rectangular one—see Figure 2) on the horizontal ruler or using Format → Paragraph → Indents and
  Spacing → Left.

- Set the first line indent by pressing Tab to move to
  the next tab stop or dragging the First Line Indent
  marker on the horizontal ruler to the desired location. You can also use Format → Paragraph →
  Indents and Spacing → Special → First Line option to
  set an exact measurement for the first line indent.

- Set the right indent by dragging the Right Indent
  marker on the ruler or set exact measurements using
  Format → Paragraph → Indents and Spacing → Right.

- Set the hanging indent (which controls all but the
  first line) by dragging the Hanging Indent marker or
  using Format → Paragraph → Indents and Spacing →
  Special → Hanging.

Change the line spacing between and within paragraphs?

Format → Paragraph → Indents and Spacing; use the
Before option to set the blank space before a paragraph,
After to set the space following the paragraph, and Line
Spacing to set the distance between lines within the para-
graph.

Set tab stops?

Use the horizontal ruler (see Figure 2 in Part 1) to select
the type of tab stop to place and then click the ruler to
place stops.

Format → Tabs to show exact locations of existing tab
stops. Type in a new location (in the default measurement

unit), choose an alignment for the type of tab stop, and click Set to create a new tab stop.

To change a tab stop, use Format → Tabs and select a tab stop. Change any options and click Set to modify the stop. Click Clear to remove a tab stop or Clear all to remove all customized stops.

Change the default spacing between tab stops?
> Format → Tabs → Default Tab Stops.

Set up a leader (such as dashed lines) between tab stops?
> Format → Tabs → Leader.

Show line numbers in a document?
> Line numbers are displayed only in Print Layout view (Page Layout in Word 97).
>
> 1. Select View → Print Layout.
> 2. Go to File → Page Setup → Layout → Line Numbers.
> 3. Select "Add line numbering" and set numbering options.

Skip line numbering for specific paragraphs?
> Select the paragraphs, then select Format → Paragraph → Line and Page Breaks → Suppress line numbers.

Working with Formats and Styles

How do I...

Determine the formats used on a paragraph or character?
> In Word 2002, select the paragraph or the specific characters, then go to Format → Reveal Formatting. You can also use Help → What's This? (or Shift-F1) and then click the text. The Reveal Formatting pane shows font, paragraph, and section formatting that applies to the selection.
>
> In Word 97 and 2000, use Help → What's This? (or Shift-F1) and click the text for a pop-up description of formatting.

Select all text in a document with the same formatting?

Make a selection or place the insertion point in the appropriate location, then choose Format → Styles and Formatting → Select All.

Right-click a selection or location and choose Select Text With Similar Formatting from the shortcut menu.

Remove formatting or styles from selected text?

Select the text and then select Clear Formatting from the Style drop-down list.

Select the text and press Ctrl-Space.

Copy formatting to another selection?

Select the text or paragraph with the formatting you want to copy. Click the Format Painter button on the Standard toolbar. Drag the pointer over the selection to which you want to copy the formatting.

TIP

Double-click the Format Painter button to have it stay down while you "paint" formatting onto multiple other selections. Click the button again to release it.

Apply consistent sets of formatting using a character style?

Character styles are collections of formats that affect characters within a paragraph and override any similar formatting placed at the paragraph level. Apply a character style by opening the Styles drop-down list on the toolbar or (in Word 2002) Format → Styles and Formatting, and then choosing a style. Character styles have an underlined "a" next to them in the drop-down toolbar list and the Styles dialog.

Apply consistent sets of formatting using a paragraph style?

Paragraph styles affect the formatting of entire paragraphs, and can hold the same kinds of formatting as a character style and more. Apply a paragraph style using the Styles drop-down list or in Word 2002 using Format → Styles and Formatting. Paragraph styles have a paragraph mark next to them in the drop-down toolbar list and the Styles dialog.

Modify a style?

In Word 2002, use Format → Styles and Formatting; click the arrow next to the style you want to change (or right-click the style) and click Modify. Use the dialog to alter the format. Select whether you want to save the file to the template attached to the document and whether you want the style automatically updated whenever you apply manual formatting to a paragraph using the style.

In Word 97 and 2000, use Format → Style; select a style from the list and click Modify.

Rename a style?

Tools → Templates and Add-Ins → Organizer → Styles. In the list on the left, select the style and click Rename.

Create a new style?

In Word 2002, use Format → Styles and Formatting → New Style.

In Word 97 and 2000, use Format → Style → New.

Delete a style?

In Word 2002, use Format → Styles and Formatting; click the arrow next to a style and choose Delete. In Word 97 and 2000, use Format → Style; select a style and click Delete. If you delete a style that you created, Word applies the Normal style to all paragraphs using that style.

In all versions, you can also use Tools → Templates and Add-Ins → Organizer; select one or more styles from the list on the left and click Delete.

Always have one paragraph style follow another?

Format → Styles and Formatting (or Format → Style in Word 97 and 2000); click a style and choose Modify. Choose a style from the "Style for following paragraph" drop-down list.

Automatically update a style when you apply manual formatting to a paragraph using that style?

Format → Styles and Formatting (or Format → Style in Word 97 and 2000); click a style and choose Modify. Select the Automatically update option.

Preview styles used in a template?

Format → Themes → Style Gallery (Format → Style Gallery in Word 97). Select a template to show what the current document will look like with styles from that template. Select the Example option to see the styles in an example document. Select the Style samples option to see an example of each style in the template. Clicking OK copies all styles from the template to the current document.

Copy styles between documents or templates?

Tools → Templates and Add-Ins → Organizer → Styles. Use the two "Styles available in" drop-down lists (Figure 9) to choose the two documents (or templates) you want to manage styles for. Styles are shown in the lists above. Select one or more styles in one document and click Copy to copy them to the other open document.

NOTE

You can manage AutoText entries, toolbars, and macros the same way as styles using the other tabs on the Organizer dialog.

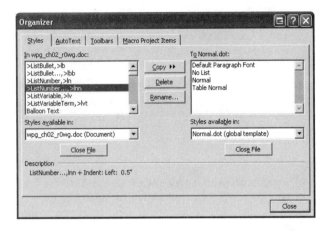

Figure 9. Organizing styles

> ***Show style names to the left of a document?***
> Tools → Options → View; set the "Style area width" value to anything other than zero.

02+ *Have Word track formatting changes in a document?*
Tools → Options → Edit → Keep track of formatting. Formatting changes are shown along with tracked changes. See "Collaborating" later in this part.

Have Word show formatting marks?
Tools → Options → View; select options from the "Formatting marks" section (Nonprinting characters section in Word 97). Selecting the All option is the same as using the Show/Hide button on the Standard toolbar. Even when the Show/Hide button is not turned on, individually selected format options are shown in the document.

02+ *Have Word mark inconsistencies in formatting?*

Tools → Options → Edit → Mark formatting inconsistencies. Inconsistent formatting (such as some headings that use bold and some that do not) are marked with squiggly blue underlines. Right-click an inconsistency for suggestions.

Have Word format a document automatically?

Format → AutoFormat. Select "AutoFormat now" to format the document all at once using current AutoFormat options. Select AutoFormat and review each change to format the entire document and then give you the chance to accept or reject each change.

Change the options Word uses for AutoFormat?

Format → AutoFormat → Options or Tools → AutoCorrect Options → AutoFormat.

Change the options Word uses to automatically format while you type?

Tools → AutoCorrect Options → AutoFormat as you Type.

00+ *Use Click and Type to automatically format text and graphics?*

Use View → Print Layout or View → Web Layout. Click somewhere in a blank area of the document where you want to enter text. The pointer changes shape as you move it to show how the text will be formatted (shown in Figure 10). When the pointer indicates the kind of text you want to enter, double-click and start typing.

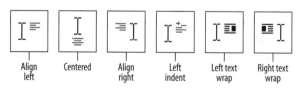

| Align left | Centered | Align right | Left indent | Left text wrap | Right text wrap |

Figure 10. Click and Type options

Creating Lists

How do I...

Create a basic bulleted or numbered list?

Type a bullet symbol (asterisk or hyphen or number), followed by a space, followed by text. Press Enter and Word formats the list automatically.

Click the Numbering or Bullets button on the Formatting toolbar.

Create a list with a different bulleting or numbering style?

Format → Bullets and Numbering; select the Bulleted, Numbered, or Outline Numbered tab depending on your need, select the type of bullet or number to use, and then click OK.

Use a picture, character, or symbol as a bullet?

Format → Bullets and Numbering → Bullets; choose a bullet character. Click Font to change font properties or click Character (Bullet in Word 97) to use a symbol or character. In Word 2000 or 2002, click Picture to use a clip art bullet.

Change the positioning of bullets and bulleted text?

Format → Bullets and Numbering → Bullets → Customize; change the values in the Bullet Position and Text Position sections.

Change the indentation of one or more lines in a list?

Select the lines and click the Decrease Indent or Increase Indent buttons on the Formatting toolbar.

Select the lines and press Tab or Shift-Tab.

Reset a list to use the default bulleting or numbering style?

Format → Bullets and Numbering → Reset.

Restart the numbering on a list instead of continuing numbering from the previous list?

Format → Bullets and Numbering → Numbered → Restart Numbering.

In Word 2000 or 2002, right-click the first line in the list and choose Restart Numbering.

Continue the numbering from a previous list?

Format → Bullets and Numbering → Numbered → Continue previous list.

In Word 2000 or 2002, right-click the first line in the list and choose Continue Numbering.

Start a numbered list using a particular number?

Format → Bullets and Numbering → Numbered → Customize → Start at.

Adjust the number style and position in a numbered list?

Format → Bullets and Numbering → Numbered → Customize.

Turn off automatic bulleting and numbering?

Tools → AutoCorrect Options → AutoFormat As You Type; select the Automatic bulleted lists and Automatic numbered lists options.

Combine multiple lists into a single list?

Select a list, choose Edit → Copy or Edit → Cut, place the insertion point in the line below the list you want to add to, and then choose Edit → Paste.

Working with Borders and Background Colors

How do I...

Apply or change a border for a paragraph, selected text, or a table?

Format → Borders and Shading → Borders. Choose a type of border, a line style and color, and click OK to apply the border. Click the buttons around the preview to turn on or off individual borders.

Apply or change page borders for all pages in a document or section?

Format → Borders and Shading → Page Borders; this works the same as regular borders, but applies borders to all pages in a section or the whole document.

Shade a paragraph or selected text with a color or pattern?

Format → Borders and Shading → Shading. Select a fill color or pattern, and choose whether to apply it to a paragraph, table element, or selected text.

Change the case of a selection?

Format → Change Case; choose a case type.

Shift-F3 to cycle through case types.

NOTE

Use Tools → AutoCorrect Options → AutoCorrect to modify whether Word automatically applies corrections to various case situations.

Set a background color for a document used as a Web page?

Format → Background; select a color from the palette or choose More Colors.

02+ *Set a background watermark for a printed document?*

Format → Background → Printed Watermark.

Set a theme for a document?
> Format → Theme. Select a theme from the list to see examples of the styles it uses. Click OK to copy all styles to the current document.

Changing Your View

This section includes tasks on changing the Word display— whether Word uses the single document interface (where a window is shown for each open document) or the multiple document interface, how a document is displayed, and some options for what is shown in the document.

How do I...

Change whether Word shows a separate window for each document?
> Tools → Options → View → Windows in Taskbar. Enable this option to show each open document in a different window and with a different button on the taskbar (this is called the single document interface).

Manage multiple windows using the single document interface?
> Click a document's button on the Windows taskbar to switch to that document. Right-click the taskbar button for other window options (minimize, maximize, etc.)

NOTE

If you are using Windows XP, multiple taskbar buttons of the same type may be grouped under a single button. Click the button to see the individual buttons for open documents. Change this grouping behavior using Start → Control Panel → Taskbar and Start Menu → Group similar Taskbar buttons.

Manage multiple windows using either document interface?
> Window → *document name* to switch to that document.

Ctrl-F6 to switch to the next open document. Ctrl-Shift-F6 to switch to the previous open document.

Create an additional window of an open document?
Window → New Window; the original window is labeled with the document name followed by a :1 and the copy is labeled :2. You can scroll to different places in each window, view each window in a different view or zoom level, and drag items between the windows.

Split an existing window for two views of a single document?
Window → Split or drag the split handle above the vertical scroll bar.

02+ *Keep the task pane from showing every time I start Word?*
Tools → Options → View → Startup Task Pane.

Switch between the four basic document views?
Select a view from the View menu or click a view button to the left of the horizontal scroll bar. Views include:

- *Normal* provides a larger workspace, but you must rely on the Status bar to see where you are in the document. One plus to working in Normal view is that page and section breaks are more visible, represented by a horizontal line and text indicating the type of break.

- *Web Layout (Online Layout in Word 97)* shows any background color or graphic (Format → Background) added to the page and shows the position of text and graphics as they should appear in a web browser. In Word 2000 and 2002, use File → Web Page Preview to open the document in your default browser for a better idea of how it will look.

- *Print Layout (Page Layout in Word 97)* adds an extra vertical ruler on the left side of the page and allows you to see the physical edges of the paper, a major help in laying out a document and monitoring pagination.

- *Outline* displays the document as a hierarchical list of headings and supporting paragraph text. Use this view for planning and structuring document headings.

Set options for using the different views?

Tools → Options → View.

In Word 2000 and 2002, options in the Print and Web Layout section include:

- *Drawings* turns on or off the display of objects created with Word's drawing tools.
- *Object Anchors* indicates the paragraphs to which objects are anchored.
- *Text Boundaries* displays dotted lines on the screen around page margins.
- *White space between pages* displays the space between the top of the text and the top edge of the page.
- *Vertical Ruler* turns on or off the vertical ruler display.

In Word 2000 and 2002, the following options are grouped into a Normal and Outline section. In Word 97, they are on different places on the View tab:

- *Wrap to window* wraps text from one line to the next based on the size of the document window rather than on the location of the margins.
- *Draft font* substitutes a single font for all different fonts in a document, speeding up the display of long documents with multiple fonts.
- *Style area width* shows style names to the left of the page margin.

2+ *Open a task pane manually?*

View → Task Pane.

Add or remove a toolbar from the display?

View → Toolbars or right-click anywhere in the toolbar area for a list of common toolbars.

Tools → Customize → Toolbars for a list of all toolbars available in Word.

Hide or show the rulers?

View → Ruler.

> ### Use a heading-based document map to navigate a document?
>
> View → Document Map to open a map of headings to the left of the document. Click any heading to jump to that location in the document window.

Get a full-screen view of your documents?

View → Full Screen hides all menus, toolbars, scroll bars, and the status bar. Click Close Full Screen on the pop-up command bar or press Esc to exit full-screen mode.

`00+` *Preview what a document will look like when published as a web page?*

File → Web Page Preview to open your default web browser and display the current document.

Zoom to different levels on a document?

Select or type a zoom level in the Zoom box on the Standard toolbar.

Select View → Zoom to open a dialog with the same functionality.

Speed up the display of a document by not showing pictures?

Tools → Options → View → Picture Placeholders. Empty frames that are the same size as the hidden pictures are displayed in the document.

`02+` *Turn off the smart tags that appear beneath text?*

Tools → Options → View → Smart Tags.

Set other options for what is shown in a document view?

Tools → Options → View.

Controlling the Flow of a Document

The following tasks show you how to control the way Word breaks and paginates pages, and how to use section breaks, headers and footers, and columns.

Working with Breaks

How do I...

Show page and other breaks in the document window?
> In Normal view, page and section breaks show at all times as dashed lines. In Print Layout (Page Layout in Word 97), page breaks appear as splits in the pages and no break codes appear. To see actual breaks in Print Layout view, use the Show/Hide button on the Standard toolbar or choose Tools → Options → View → All.

Insert a manual page break?
> Insert → Break → Page Break or press Ctrl-Enter.

Prevent automatic page breaks within paragraphs?
> Select the paragraph and choose Format → Paragraph → Line and Page Breaks → Keep Lines Together.

Prevent an automatic page break between a paragraph and the following paragraph?
> Select the first paragraph and choose Format → Paragraph → Line and Page Breaks → Keep with next.

Force a page break directly before a paragraph?
> Select the paragraph and choose Format → Paragraph → Line and Page Breaks → Page break before.

Prevent Word from printing the first or last line of a paragraph on a page by itself?
> Select the paragraph and choose Format → Paragraph → Line and Page Breaks → Widow/Orphan control.

End a line of text and force it to continue beneath an object?
    Insert → Break → Text wrapping break.

Create a new section without starting a new page?
    Insert → Break → Continuous.

Insert a break and start the new section on the next page?
    Insert → Break → Next page.

Insert a break and start the new section on the next odd- or even-numbered page?
    Insert → Break; choose Even page or Odd page.

Columns

How do I...

Create or remove columns?
    Select View → Print Layout (Page Layout in Word 97). Select the text you want to format as a column (or that you want to remove column formatting from), click the Columns button on the Standard toolbar, and select the number of columns you want. Select one column to remove existing columns.

Add a vertical line between columns?
    Place the insertion point in the section with columns you want vertical lines between and select Format → Columns → Line between.

Change the width of a column?
    Place the insertion point in the section with the columns you want to change. Drag the column markers on the horizontal ruler to move columns (Figure 11).

Create a heading that spans multiple columns?
    Type the heading text at the beginning of the leftmost column and press Enter. Select the heading text, click the Columns button, and make it one column. For a better heading effect, create a border around the new heading paragraph. (See "Formatting.")

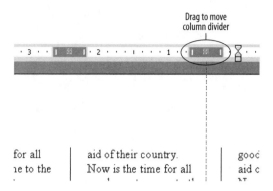

Figure 11. Drag a column handle to size columns

Insert a column break to force a new column to start?

Place the insertion point where you want the new column to start and choose Insert → Break → Column break.

Show column boundaries?

Tools → Options → View → Text Boundaries.

Headers and Footers

How do I...

Edit a header or footer?

View → Header and Footer. This places your view in the header box for the current page (where you can type or insert text and graphics) and opens the Header and Footer toolbar (Figure 12).

Insert a chapter number and title into a header or footer?

First, you must divide a document into sections that represent chapters. At the beginning of each section, you must make a heading (using one of the default heading

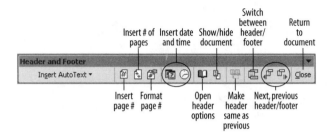

Figure 12. Controlling headers and footers

styles) with the chapter number and title. Once this is done, use the following steps in each chapter:

1. Click View → Header and Footer.
2. Make sure each section is made the same as the previous section.
3. Place the insertion point in the header where you want the chapter number and title to go.
4. Select Insert → Reference → Cross-reference (Insert → Cross-Reference in Word 97).
5. Select Heading from the Reference Type drop-down list.
6. From the list, select the heading that contains the chapter information.
7. Select Heading number from the Insert reference to drop-down list and click Insert to insert the chapter number.
8. Select Heading text from the Insert reference to drop-down list and click Insert to insert the chapter title.

Make the first page header or footer different from other pages?

File → Page Setup → Layout → Different first page. Once you've done this, go to the first page and create a different header or footer.

Make headers or footers different for odd and even pages?

File → Page Setup → Layout → Different odd and even. Once you've done this, go to the header on an even page and set it up, then do the same for an odd page.

Make headers or footers different for different sections of a document?

Place the insertion point in the section you want to change. Select View → Header and Footer. On the Header and Footer toolbar, if the Same as Previous button is enabled, click it to break the connection to the previous section. Edit the header or footer.

Make a header or footer the same as the ones in the previous section?

Place the insertion point in the section you want to change. Select View → Header and Footer. On the Header and Footer toolbar, if the Same as Previous button is not enabled, click it to delete the current header and establish a connection to the previous section.

Adjust the position of a header or footer?

To change the distance from the edge of the page and a header or footer, choose File → Page Setup → Layout and adjust the Header and Footer values.

To change the distance of a header or footer from the text on the page, choose View → Header and Footer, move to the header or footer you want to adjust, and then use the margin boundaries on the vertical ruler to adjust the size of the header or footer.

Inserting Fields and Reference Items

The following solutions show how to insert fields, use reference items like tables of contents and indexes, and insert and control pictures, diagrams, and other objects.

Working with Fields

How do I...

Insert a field?

In Word 2000 and 2002, use Insert → Field; choose a field from the list, select additional properties and click OK to insert the field. Click Field Codes to enter field codes directly.

In Word 97, use Insert → Field; choose a category and field name. Fill in the field codes directly or click Options to set additional properties.

NOTE

The Word help files contain a complete reference of fields and field codes. You can browse their contents using the Help window or right-click any field in the Field dialog and choose What's This? to jump straight to that field's help file description.

00+ *Edit a field?*

Right-click the field and choose Edit Field.

Show the field code instead of the field results?

To switch between showing results and code for a single field, select the field and press Shift-F9.

To switch between results and codes for all fields in a document, press Alt-F9.

Shade fields to make them stand out?

Tools → Options → View → Field Shading; you can have fields always shaded, never shaded, or shaded only when selected.

Lock or unlock a field?

Locking a field prevents its results from being updated. To lock a field, select it and press Ctrl-F11. To unlock a field, press Ctrl-Shift-F11.

Update a field?
    Select the field and press F9.

Update all fields in a document?
    Choose Edit → Select All (Ctrl-A), and then press F9.

Have Word automatically update all fields before printing?
    Tools → Options → Print → Update fields.

Change a field result to normal text?
    Select the field and press Ctrl-Shift-F9.

Footnotes and Endnotes

How do I...

Insert a footnote or endnote?
    To insert and format the first note, use Insert → Reference → Footnote (or Insert → Footnote in Word 97 and 2000); select footnotes or endnotes, choose a number format, and click Insert.

    To insert subsequent notes using the same format as the first note, press Ctrl-Alt-F for footnotes or Ctrl-Alt-D for endnotes.

Change how footnotes or endnotes are numbered?
    In Word 2002, place the insertion point in the section in which you want to change the format (all notes in a section must be formatted the same way) and choose Insert → Reference → Footnote. Change the format, choose whether to apply changes to the current section or to the whole document, and click Apply.

    In Word 97 and 2000, use Insert → Footnote → Options to make the same changes.

Change the placement of footnotes or endnotes?
    Insert → Reference → Footnote; select Footnotes or Endnotes, change the location using the drop-down list, choose whether to apply changes to the current section or to the whole document, and click Apply.

In Word 97 and 2000, use Insert → Footnote → Options to make changes.

View the text of a footnote or endnote without scrolling to it?
Hold the pointer over the reference mark for a moment to show a pop-up with the note text.

Change the separator used for footnotes or endnotes?
Select View → Normal then select View → Footnotes to open the note area (if you have footnotes and endnotes, you'll get a message asking which to view). In the note area, use the drop-down list to select the Footnote (or Endnote) Separator. You can delete the line shown or replace it with other text, drawing, or picture.

Create a footnote or endnote continuation notice?
Select View → Normal and then select View → Footnotes. Use the drop-down list to select Footnote (or Endnote) Continuation Notice. In the window, enter the text that should appear when a footnote or endnote continues onto another page.

Delete a footnote or endnote?
Select the reference mark (and not the note text) for the note you want to delete, and then press Backspace or Delete. Word renumbers the remaining notes.

Move a footnote or endnote?
Select the reference mark for the note and use any method for moving (drag the selection or use Edit → Cut) or copying (hold Ctrl while dragging or use Edit → Copy). Word renumbers the notes if necessary.

Convert a footnote to an endnote or vice versa?
Scroll to the footnote or endnote text, right-click a note, and choose the convert command. You can also right-click note text in the Footnote area that opens when you choose View → Footnotes in Normal view.

Convert all footnotes to endnotes or vice versa?
Insert → Reference → Footnote → Convert (Insert → Footnote → Options → Convert in Word 97 and 2000).

Use a footnote or endnote more than once?

Insert → Reference → Cross-Reference (Insert → Cross-Reference in Word 97 and 2000). In the Reference type box, choose Footnote or Endnote. In the For Which box, choose the note you want to refer to. In the Insert reference to box, click Footnote number or Endnote number. Click Insert.

Cross-References, Captions, and Bookmarks

How do I...

Create a cross-reference to another item in a document?

Insert → Reference → Cross-Reference (Insert → Cross-Reference in Word 97 and 2000). Choose a reference type (heading, figure, etc.), where the reference should lead, and then pick the exact reference target from the list.

Change the target of a cross-reference?

Click the cross-reference field and select Insert → Reference → Cross-Reference (Insert → Cross-Reference in Word 97 and 2000). Change the target of the cross-reference and click Insert.

Update cross-references in a document?

If a cross-reference refers to a specific location in the document (e.g., "see page 45") and the page number changes, right-click the cross-reference field and select Update Field. You can also click the reference and press F9.

Update all cross-references in a document by selecting Edit → Select All (or Ctrl-A) and then pressing F9.

Add a caption to a table, figure, or other object?

Select the item and use Insert → Reference → Caption (Insert → Caption in Word 97 and 2000) or right-click the item and choose Caption from the shortcut menu. Type a caption, choose the type of item from the Label drop-down list, choose a position (above or below the item), and click Insert.

Have Word automatically add captions when you insert objects?

Insert → Reference → Caption → AutoCaption (Insert → Caption → AutoCaption in Word 97 and 2000). In the AutoCaption dialog, choose the items that should automatically get captions, and choose a label type and position for each type of item.

Change the label of a caption?

Delete the existing caption and insert a new caption.

Change the label of all similar captions?

Select one of the captions and choose Insert → Reference → Caption (Insert → Caption in Word 97 and 2000). Click Label to change the label name, make any other changes, and then click Insert to change all captions.

Change the numbering of captions?

Select a caption, then use Insert → Reference → Caption → Numbering. In Word 97 and 2000, use Insert → Caption → Numbering.

Include a chapter number in a caption?

First, you must create a section for each chapter and format the chapter title using one of Word's built-in heading styles. Then use Insert → Reference → Caption → Numbering → Include chapter number. In Word 97 and 2000, use Insert → Caption → Numbering → Include chapter number.

Create a table of figures using captions in the document?

In Word 2002, Insert → Reference → Index and Tables → Table of Figures.

In Word 97 and 2000, Insert → Index and Tables → Table of Figures.

Add a bookmark?

Place the insertion point or make a selection and then use Insert → Bookmark. Bookmarks are used to mark locations for future reference.

Delete a bookmark?

Insert → Bookmark; choose a bookmark and click Delete.

Go to a bookmark?

Insert → Bookmark; select a bookmark and click Go To.

Edit → Goto (or Ctrl-G); select Bookmarks in the Go To What list, choose a specific bookmark and click Go To.

`00+` *Show or hide bookmarks in a document?*

Tools → Options → View → Bookmarks. Bookmarks are shown with light grey brackets around them.

Tables and Indexes

How do I...

Create a table of contents?

Place the insertion point where you want to insert the table of contents and use Insert → Reference → Index and Tables → Table of Contents (or Insert → Index and Tables → Table of Contents in Word 97 and 2000). Select options and format and click OK. The table of contents is inserted as a single field and is based on the headings in a document (paragraphs that use the built-in heading styles).

Make a table of contents use some heading levels, but not others?

Insert → Reference → Index and Tables → Table of Contents → Options (or Insert → Index and Tables → Table of Contents in Word 97 and 2000). Make sure that the Styles option is selected and the Outline Levels option is turned off. Enter the table of contents level you want to use in the box for each heading level and leave the boxes empty for heading levels you don't want to use. For example, to skip headings formatted with the Heading 1 style, leave that box blank and enter a "1" in the box for the Heading 2 style, "2" in the box for the Heading 3 style, and so on.

Mark a special entry to be included in a table of contents, even if it's not a heading?

Select entry and press Alt-Shift-O; name the entry, select the table of contents it should be used in (if you have more than one), and choose the level at which the entry should appear.

When you create the table of contents, you must make sure the Table Entry Fields option is selected in the Options dialog (Insert → Reference → Indexes and Tables → Table of Contents → Options).

Update a table of contents?

Select the table and press F9.

To have a table of contents updated automatically before printing, use Tools → Options → Print → Update Fields.

Delete a table of contents?

Select the table of contents and press Delete.

In Outline View (View → Outline), you can click the Go To TOC button on the Outlining toolbar and then press Delete.

Make the table of contents appear instead of {TOC}?

This happens when the field code is displayed instead of the field results. Right-click the field and choose Toggle Field Codes.

Fix page numbers and missing headings in my table of contents?

These problems usually occur when a document has been changed and the table of contents has not been updated. Select the table and press F9.

Change the format used in my table of contents?

The best way to change a table of contents is to delete it and build a new one.

You can also change the formatting styles used in a table of contents. In Word 2002, choose Format → Styles and Formatting and then click a line in the table of contents near the number. A TOC style (TOC1, TOC2, etc.) appears in the "Formatting of Selected Text" box. Right-click the style and choose Modify.

In Word 97 and 2000, use Format → Styles → Modify.

Mark a citation for use in a table of authorities?

A table of authorities lists the references in a legal document. To create a table of authorities, you must mark citations in the document and then build the table. To mark a citation, do the following:

1. Select the first long citation in your document and press Alt-Shift-I.

2. In the Selected Text box, change the long citation to appear the way you want it in the table of authorities.

3. Select a Category from the drop-down list.

4. In the Short Citation box, enter the short version for the citation that is used in the rest of the document.

5. Click Mark to mark a single citation or Mark All to mark all citations that match the text in the Short Citation box.

Remove a citation from a table of authorities?

Click Show/Hide on the Standard toolbar to show field codes. To the right of a citation, you'll see a TA field (e.g., { TA \s "*citation*" }). Delete the entire field.

Create a table of authorities using marked citations?

Place the insertion point where you want to build the table. Use Insert → Reference → Index and Tables → Table of Authorities (or Insert → Index and Tables → Table of Authorities in Word 97 and 2000).

Update a table of authorities?

Select the table and press F9.

To update the table automatically before printing, select Tools → Options → Print → Update Fields.

Create or modify categories of citations?

Alt-Shift-I → Category; click a category (unused categories are named 8–16) and type a name in the Replace With box.

Mark a selection to be included in an index?

Select a word or phrase and press Alt-Shift-X. In the Main Entry box, type the entry as it should appear in the index. Enter text in the Subentry box to mark the selection as a subentry in the index. Choose whether the page number for the entry should be boldfaced or italicized and click Mark. Click Mark All to mark all instances of that word the same way.

To create an index entry without using preselected text, just place the insertion point and press Alt-Shift-X.

Mark long entries that span more than one page to be included in an index?

Select the text to be marked and create a bookmark. Then press Alt-Shift-X, configure the entry, and select the Page Range option. Choose the bookmark to reference and click Mark.

Create an index entry that refers to another entry?

Press Alt-Shift-X, configure the entry, and select the Cross-Reference option. Type the text for the cross-reference (e.g., "See Bicycle") and click Mark.

Change how a marked entry will appear in the index?

Index entries are marked by placing a field to the right of the marked phrase (e.g., { XE "Bicycle:Repair" }). If you don't see the fields, click the Show/Hide button on the Standard toolbar. Select the text inside the quotes and replace or format it to change the index entry.

Delete an index entry?

Select the entire index field to the right of the marked phrase and delete it.

Create an index?

Place the insertion point where the index will go and select Insert → Reference → Index and Tables → Index (or Insert → Index and Tables → Index in Word 97 and 2000). Select configuration options and click OK.

Modify the styles used for entries in an index?

In Word 2002, Insert → Reference → Index and Tables → Index → Modify.

In Word 97 and 2000, Insert → Index and Tables → Index → Modify.

Have Word automatically mark index entries using a concordance file?

A *concordance file* is a separate document with a two-column table that lists phrases to search for in a document in the first column and the entries to place in the index in the second column (in the format *entry:subentry*). Create a new file, create the table, and then save the file.

In the document you want to index, select Insert → Reference → Index and Tables → Index → AutoMark (Insert → Index and Tables → Index → AutoMark in Word 97 and 2000). Select the concordance file and click Open. Word searches the document and marks the first occurrence in a paragraph of any word in the first column as an index entry.

Working with Hyperlinks

How do I...

Create a hyperlink?

Select text or object, or just place the insertion point, and select Insert → Hyperlink (or Ctrl-K). In the Link To list, choose a target (existing file, web page, another place in

the document, and so on). Configure the hyperlink and
click OK.

Remove a hyperlink, but keep the text?
> In Word 2000 or 2002, right-click the hyperlink in the
> document window and select Remove Hyperlink.
>
> In Word 97, right-click the hyperlink and select Hyper-
> link → Edit Hyperlink → Remove Link.

Change a hyperlink?
> Right-click the hyperlink and choose Edit Hyperlink (or
> Hyperlink → Edit Hyperlink in Word 97).

Follow a hyperlink found in a document?
> In Word 2000 and 2002, hold Ctrl and click the link.
>
> In Word 97, click the link.

00+ *Change how hyperlinks are followed?*
> Tools → Options → Edit; disable the Use Ctrl+Click to
> follow hyperlink option and you can follow a hyperlink
> just by clicking it.

Set a hyperlink base that all hyperlinks in a document will use?
> File → Properties → Summary; type a base in the Hyper-
> link base box.

Inserting Objects

The following tasks show you how to insert objects into your
document, including pictures, drawings, charts, and information from other types of documents.

Clip Art, Drawings, and Pictures

How do I...

Insert a piece of clip art?
> Insert → Picture → ClipArt.
>
> In Word 2002, the Insert Clip Art task pane is used
> instead; enter a part of the file name and click Search.

The Other Search Options section lets you specify where to search and the types of files to search for. By default, the search returns clip art, pictures, video, and sound files.

In Word 97 and 2000, a dialog box opens with tools for finding and inserting clip art.

Use the Clip Organizer to browse clip art and other media?
In Word 2002, use Insert → Picture → ClipArt → Clip Organizer. In Word 97 and 2000, use Insert → Picture → Clip Art. Select a folder from the collection list to see thumbnail previews in the right pane.

Add a clip to the Clip Organizer?
In Word 2002, use Insert → Picture → ClipArt → Clip Organizer. In the Clip Organizer window, use the File → Add Clips to Organizer menu for options on adding clips.

In Word 97 and 2000, use Insert → Picture → Clip Art → Import Clips.

View the properties and a preview of a clip before inserting?
Right-click a clip's thumbnail, and then choose Preview/Properties.

Find more clips online?
Insert → Picture → ClipArt → Clips Online; this opens Microsoft's Design Gallery in your default web browser.

Insert a picture from a file?
Insert → Picture → From File; find the file and click Insert. This action embeds the picture, which increases the document's size.

Link a picture to a file?
Insert → Picture → From File; find the file. In Word 2000 and 2002, click the down arrow next to the Insert button, and choose Link to File. In Word 97, select the "Link to file" option and click Insert. The picture is displayed, but not embedded. Changes to the original picture file are reflected in the document.

Retrieve a picture from a scanner or camera?
> Insert → Picture → From Scanner or Camera.

Create an organizational chart?
> In Word 2002, Insert → Picture → Organization Chart or Insert → Diagram → Organization Chart; this creates a basic hierarchical organization chart and opens an Organization Chart toolbar (Figure 13).

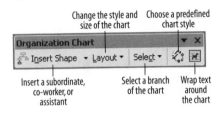

Figure 13. Creating an organization chart

> In Word 97 and 2000, insert an organization chart as an object using Insert → Object → Create New; select Organization Chart from the Object type box.

02+ *Create a diagram?*
> Insert → Diagram; select a basic diagram (cycle, pyramid, target, and so on). Use the Diagram toolbar to change styles and add shapes.

02+ *Create another type of drawing or picture?*
> Insert → Picture → New Drawing. Use the Drawing toolbar (Figure 14) to add components to a blank drawing canvas.

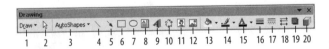

Figure 14. Use the Drawing toolbar to create many different elements

In Figure 14 are the following elements:

1. Holds commands for grouping, ordering, arranging, and moving shapes in the drawing.
2. Provides a pointer for selecting shapes.
3. Inserts various types of predefined shapes (lines, arrows, flowchart symbols) and is the same as using the Insert → Picture → AutoShapes command.

4-7. Tools for drawing a line, arrow, rectangle, and circle.

8. Inserts a text box.
9. Inserts WordArt (predefined shapes and shadows applied to your own text). This is the same as using the Insert → Picture → WordArt command.
10. Inserts a diagram or organization chart (same as Insert → Diagram or Insert → Picture → Organization chart).
11. Same as using Insert → Picture → ClipArt.
12. Same as using Insert → Picture → From File.
13. Changes the fill color for the selected object.
14. Changes the line color for the selected object.
15. Changes text color.

16-18. Changes line style, dash style, and arrow style.

19. Changes shadowing of selected object.
20. Changes 3-D effect of selected object.

02+ *Specify whether a drawing canvas is automatically inserted around AutoShapes when I create them?*

Tools → Options → General → Automatically create drawing canvas when inserting AutoShapes.

Create a chart based on a table of information?

Insert → Picture → Chart. A chart object is inserted in the document and a separate window opens with a datasheet. Fill out the data (or change or add headings) to update the chart. If you close the datasheet, you can double-click the chart at any time to reactivate it. While the chart is active, Word's menus change to hold commands for editing and formatting the chart. Some of these commands include:

- View → Datasheet to reopen the separate datasheet window.
- Insert → Cells to create new cells in the datasheet.
- The Format menu lets you change the font, number style, and placement of the chart.
- Tools → Options changes very basic datasheet and chart settings.
- Chart → Chart Type lets you select the type of chart (bar, pie, line, etc.).
- Chart → Chart Options lets you change titles, axes, gridlines, legends, and data labels.

TIP

If you have Microsoft Excel, a more powerful (and often easier) solution than using Word's limited chart feature is to create a worksheet and chart in Excel and then insert that into Word. This is covered a bit later in this section.

Text Boxes

How do I...

Create a text box?
> Insert → Text Box or click the Text Box button on the Drawing toolbar. In Word 97, you must draw the text box by dragging.

Create a text box around existing text?
> Select the text and choose Insert → Text Box.

Link a text box to another text box to continue a story?
> Select the first text box, click the Create Text Box Link button on the Text Box toolbar, and then click another, empty text box. Text that does not fit into the first text box is automatically continued in the next linked text box, and text is automatically moved if you resize the

text boxes. You can link any number of text boxes in this manner. Use the Next and Previous text box buttons on the toolbar to move between linked text boxes.

Break the link between two text boxes?
Select a text box and click the Break Forward Link button on the Text Box toolbar to break any link from the current text box to another. This does not affect any link that may come to the current text box from a previous text box.

Convert a text box to a frame?
Select the text box and use Format → Text Box → Text Box → Convert to Frame.

Change the direction of text in a text box?
Select the text box and click the Change Text Direction button on the Text Box toolbar.

Manipulating Objects

How do I...

Change the size of an object?
Select the object and use the drag handles at the corners and sides of the object.

To specify an exact size, select the object and use Format → *objectname* → Size.

Change the wrapping style of an object?
Select the object and use Format → *objectname* → Layout (in Word 97, Format → *objectname* → Wrapping).

Change cropping for a picture object?
Select the object and choose Format → Picture → Picture; use the controls in the Crop From section of the dialog.

Change color display settings for a picture object?
Select the object and choose Format → Picture → Picture; use the controls in the Image Control section of the dialog.

`02+` *Change resolution for a picture object?*
Select the object and use Format → Picture → Picture → Compress.

`02+` *Turn on or off compression for a picture object?*
Select the object and use Format → Picture → Picture → Compress → Compress Pictures.

Change fill and line colors for a drawing object?
Select the object and use Format → Picture → Colors and Lines.

`00+` *Add alternative web text for an object?*
Select the object and use Format → Picture → Web.

Embedding and Linking

How do I...

Insert a file into the document?
Insert → File; choose a file and click Insert. The information from the file is embedded into the Word document. Mostly, this command is good for inserting the contents of another Word file. If the file is anything other than another Word document, the information in the file is converted (if a converter is available) into Word format.

Embed an object from another file?
Insert → Object → Create from File; type or browse for the filename and click OK. The entire contents of the file are embedded into the Word document as a single object.

You can also copy an object from another open document and paste the object into an open Word document.

Create a new object?
Insert → Object → Create New; choose an object type. Double-click the object after it is inserted to edit it.

Drag objects or information between programs?
Dragging a selection (e.g., an Excel graph or selection from another Word document) into an open Word docu-

ment moves the selection there. Holding Ctrl while dragging it copies the selection there. What happens depends on the program. When dragging selections from another Word document, the selection becomes part of a document. When dragging a chart from Excel, the chart becomes a picture. When dragging a spreadsheet from Excel, it becomes a table.

Edit an embedded object from Word?

Double-click the object to edit it using commands from the object's source application. For example, double-clicking an object inserted from an Excel document provides access to Excel's menus for working with the object.

Link an object to another file?

When you link an object, it is displayed in the Word document, but not embedded. If the original object (say, an Excel chart) is updated, the updates are reflected in the Word document.

To link to an entire file, use Insert → Object → Create From File; choose the file and make sure the "Link to file" option is selected.

To link to a particular object, open the source file, copy the object, switch to the Word document, and choose Edit → Paste Special → Paste link.

Edit a linked object?

Double-click a linked object to open the source file using the application that created it.

Update a linked object manually?

Edit → Links; select the links to update and click Update Now.

Stop a linked object from updating automatically?

Edit → Links; select the link and choose the Manual update option.

Prevent a linked object from being updated?

Edit → Links; select the link and choose the Locked option.

Break the link for a linked object?

Edit → Links; select the link and click Break Link.

Reconnect a linked object after breaking it?

You must insert the linked object again; you cannot reconnect a broken link.

Have Word update linked objects automatically when I print a document?

Tools → Options → Print → Update Links.

Working with Tables

The following tasks show you how to create and edit tables.

How do I...

Create a quick table by choosing the number of rows and columns?

Click the Insert Table button on the toolbar, hold the mouse button, and drag the number of rows and columns that you want.

Draw a table to fit a particular space?

Table → Draw Table to change the pointer to the table drawing tool. Drag a rectangle to make the outer border of your table. Drag lines inside the border to form cells. This is a quick way to make irregular tables.

Create a single row table by typing out a line of columns?

Type a plus (+) followed by hyphens (-). Type an additional plus for each column marker and a final plus for the right border of the table. For example, typing "+--------------+---------------+-------------+" and pressing Enter would create a table with a single row and three roughly equal columns.

Create a table using other options?

Table → Insert → Table; choose the number of rows and columns, how the contents should fit, and click OK.

Insert columns or rows into an existing table?

In Word 2000 and 2002, place the insertion point somewhere in the table. Choose Table → Insert and then pick one of the column or row options.

In Word 97, these commands are right on the Table menu. Place an insertion point or select a row to use Table → Insert Row. Select an existing column to use Table → Insert Column.

00+ *Insert cells into an existing table?*

Place the insertion point and then use Table → Insert → Cells. Choose how to shift the existing cells in the table and click OK.

Remove columns, rows, or cells from a table?

In Word 2000 and 2002, place the insertion point in the column, row, or cell, and use the commands on the Table → Delete submenu.

In Word 97, select the column, row, or cell to delete and choose the appropriate command on the Table menu.

In Word 2000 and 2002, select a group of cells in the table and remove them by pressing Backspace or using Edit → Cut.

Delete the text in a group of cells without removing the cells?

Drag to select the cells and their text and press Delete. Do not press Backspace as this will delete the cells themselves.

Select an entire column or row?

Place the insertion point in the column or row and use Table → Select → Column or Table → Select → Row (in Word 97, these commands are right on the Table menu).

Move the pointer to the top edge of the column (it turns into a down-facing black arrow) or to the left edge of a row (it turns into an upper-right-facing arrow) and click to select the column or row.

Select a cell or group of cells?

Place the insertion point in the cell and use Table → Select → Cell (or Table → Select Cell in Word 97).

Move the pointer over the left edge of the cell (it turns into an upper-right-facing black arrow) and click to select that cell.

Drag to select a group of cells.

Select a entire table?

Place the insertion point anywhere in the table and use Table → Select → Table (or Table → Select Table in Word 97).

Merge multiple cells into a single cell?

Select the cells and use Table → Merge Cells.

Split a cell or cells into multiple other cells?

Place the insertion point in the cell (or select a group of cells) and use Table → Split Cell. Choose the number of rows and columns into which to split the cell.

Split a table between two rows?

Place the insertion point on the row that will become the top line of the second table and use Table → Split Table.

Format a table automatically?

Table → Table AutoFormat; choose a category, a table style, set options, and click OK.

Make a group of rows or columns a uniform size?

Select a group of cells in the row (or column) and use Table → AutoFit → Distribute Columns Evenly or Table → AutoFit → Distribute Rows Evenly (in Word 97, these commands appear on the Table menu).

00+ *Make a table expand automatically to fit the contents of the table?*

Table → AutoFit → AutoFit to Contents.

Make a table contract to fit the window whenever the window changes?

Table → AutoFit → AutoFit to Window.

Make the headings of the table repeat on the first line if the table crosses a page break?

Table → Heading Rows Repeat (Table → Headings in Word 97).

Convert a table to text?

Table → Convert → Table to Text; choose how to separate the text once it is converted and click OK.

Convert text to a table?

Table → Convert → Text to Table (in Word 97, Table → Text to Table); choose the number of columns and rows, the AutoFit behavior, and specify the separator used in the text that will designate where new cells begin.

Sort a table?

Table → Sort; you can sort by up to three columns in a nested sort.

Change the direction of text in a cell?

Right-click the cell and choose Text Direction. You can also select a cell and use the Text Direction button on the Tables and Borders toolbar to switch between available directions.

Create a formula that uses values in other cells?

Place the insertion point in a cell and choose Table → Formula.

Hide the gridlines for a table?

Table → Hide Gridlines.

Specify an exact size and alignment for a table?

Table → Table Properties → Table or right-click the table and choose Table Properties → Table.

Make text wrap around a table?

Table → Table Properties → Table.

Specify an exact size and alignment for a cell?
> In Word 2000 and 2002, use Table → Table Properties → Cell.
>
> In Word 97, specify the alignment using Table → Cell Height and Width → Alignment.

00+ *Change the margins used within a specific table cell?*
> Table → Table Properties → Cell → Options.

00+ *Change the default margins used for all table cells?*
> Table → Table Properties → Table → Options.

00+ *Change the space between table cells?*
> Table → Table Properties → Table → Options.

Specify an exact size for each column in a table?
> Place the insertion point in a column. In Word 2000 and 2002, use Table → Table Properties → Column. In Word 97, use Table → Cell Height and Width. Use the Next and Previous Column buttons to set each column while the dialog is still open.

Specify an exact size for each row in a table?
> Place the insertion point in a row and use Table → Table Properties → Row (Table → Cell Height and Width → Row in Word 97).

Prevent a row from breaking across a page?
> Table → Table Properties → Row (Table → Cell Height and Width → Row in Word 97); disable the "Allow row to break across pages" option.

Spelling and Other Tools

The following tasks cover Word's Spelling and other language tools, as well as printing envelopes and labels.

Spelling and Grammar

How do I...

Review misspelled words in the document window?

By default, suspect words are shown with squiggly red lines under them in the document window. Right-click a suspect word to see spelling suggestions. Double-click the Spelling and Grammar Status icon (looks like a book) on the Status bar to jump to the next misspelled word in the document and automatically open a shortcut menu with spelling suggestions.

Turn off the red and green lines under words?

Tools → Options → Spelling & Grammar (or right-click the Spelling and Grammar Status icon and choose Options). Select the "Hide spelling errors in this document" and "Hide grammatical errors in this document" options.

Turn off background spelling- and grammar-checking completely?

Tools → Options → Spelling & Grammar; disable the "Check spelling as you type" and "Check grammar as you type" options.

Perform a full spelling and grammar check?

Tools → Spelling and Grammar or F7 to open the Spelling and Grammar dialog (Figure 15), which shows errors in context along with suggested corrections.

1. *Not in Dictionary.* The name of this window changes based on the error found. "Not in Dictionary" is displayed for spelling errors. For grammatical errors, Word displays the type of error found, such as "Passive voice" or "Repeated space." Spelling errors are indicated in red text, grammatical errors in green. Use the buttons on the right to act on the error. Type a change directly in this window and click the Change button to apply custom corrections.

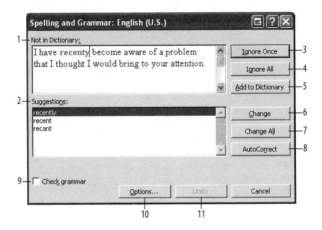

Figure 15. Check spelling and grammar for an entire document at once

2. *Suggestions.* This holds suggested corrections for the error. Select a suggestion and click the Change or Change All buttons (see #6 and 7).

3. *Ignore.* Use this button to ignore the current instance of the error. The next time the document is checked, the error is displayed again.

4. *Ignore All (Ignore Rule).* This command becomes Ignore Rule when a grammatical error is displayed. With spelling errors, this button causes Word to ignore *all* instances of the error in the document. The next time the document is checked, the errors are displayed again.

The Ignore Rule button causes Word to ignore the grammatical rule throughout the document and in all *future* checks of the document, as well. Use Tools → Options → Spelling & Grammar → Recheck Document to reset the rules for a document so that ignored rules are checked again.

5. *Add (Next Sentence)*. For spelling errors, the Add button adds the spelling of the word displayed in the Not in Dictionary window to a custom dictionary. This dictionary is named *custom.dic* by default.

   For grammatical errors, this is replaced with the Next Sentence command, which skips the current error and resumes checking with the next sentence. Use this button or the Change button to enter a custom correction in the error window.

6. *Change*. Select a correction in the Suggestions window or enter a custom correction in the error window and then click the Change button.

7. *Change All*. Available only with spelling errors, this button changes all instances of the error in the document to the selected suggestion.

8. *AutoCorrect*. This button adds the misspelled word and the selected correction to the AutoCorrect list. The next time the same error is encountered in a document, Word corrects the error as soon as it's typed in a document.

9. *Check Grammar*. Disable to have Word check only spelling errors. This option remains disabled until you enable it again.

10. *Options*. This is a shortcut to Tools → Options → Spelling & Grammar.

11. *Undo*. Reverse the last correction made.

Check only spelling and not grammar?
   Tools → Spelling and Grammar; disable the Check Grammar option.

Create a custom dictionary?
   Tools → Options → Spelling & Grammar → Custom Dictionaries → New.

Add an existing custom dictionary?
   Tools → Options → Spelling & Grammar → Custom Dictionaries → Add.

Remove a custom dictionary?

Tools → Options → Spelling & Grammar → Custom Dictionaries; select a custom dictionary and click Remove.

Change what the grammar checker looks for?

Tools → Options → Spelling & Grammar → Settings.

Recheck a document where you have previously ignored words?

Tools → Options → Spelling & Grammar → Recheck Document.

Choose whether to spell-check words in upper case, numbers, and Internet addresses?

Tools → Options → Spelling & Grammar; use the options in the Spelling section of the dialog.

Show the readability statistics for a document?

Tools → Options → Spelling & Grammar → Show Readability Statistics; do a full spell-check of the document via Tools → Spelling and Grammar; and statistics will be displayed at the end of the spell-check. This option is unavailable if grammar-checking is turned off.

Other Tools

How do I...

02+ *Translate a document or selection?*

Tools → Language → Translate. Enter text, use the current selection, or select the entire document. Choose the languages you want to translate and click Go.

Look up alternative words in the thesaurus?

Tools → Language → Thesaurus (or Shift-F7). If a word was selected, synonyms are listed. If no word was selected, type a word in the Insert box and click Look Up. Select a synonym and click Replace (if a word in the document is selected) or Insert.

Calculate the word and character count for a document?
   Tools → Word Count. Select text and use Tools → Word Count to calculate just that selection.

02+

> **See the word count on a toolbar?**
> View → Toolbars → Word Count; click Recount to display a current word count for the document or a selection.

Automatically create a summary of a document?
   Tools → AutoSummarize; choose a type of summary, the percentage of the original that should be included in the summary, and click OK.

Hyphenation

How do I...

Turn on or off automatic hyphenation of a document?
   Tools → Language → Hyphenation → Automatically Hyphenate Document.

Control options for automatic hyphenation?
   Tools → Language → Hyphenation.

Manually hyphenate a document?
   Tools → Language → Hyphenation → Manual.

Insert a non-breaking hyphen so that a hyphenated phrase is not broken at the end of a line?
   Place the insertion point where you want the hyphen and press Ctrl-Shift-Hyphen.

Insert an optional hyphen so that a word only breaks at a certain point?
   Place the insertion point where you want the hyphen and press Ctrl-Hyphen.

Remove manual hyphenation?
   Edit → Replace → More → Special → Optional Hyphen; leave the Replace with box empty and use the Find Next,

Replace, or Replace All buttons to search for and remove hyphens.

Exclude a paragraph from automatic hyphenation?
Format → Paragraph → Line and Page Breaks → Don't Hyphenate.

Letters, Envelopes, and Labels

How do I...

Create and print form letters using a list of recipients or my Outlook contact list?
In Word 2002, use Tools → Letters and Mailings → Mail Merge Wizard; select the Letters option, click Next, and follow the steps in the wizard.

In Word 97 and 2000, use Tools → Mail Merge; use the Create drop-down list to select Form Letters.

Create and print mailing labels using a list of recipients or my Outlook contact list?
In Word 2002, use Tools → Letters and Mailings → Mail Merge Wizard; select the Labels option, click Next, and follow the steps in the wizard.

In Word 97 and 2000, use Tools → Mail Merge; use the Create drop-down list to select Mailing Labels.

`02+` *Create and send form email messages using a list of recipients or my Outlook contact list?*
Tools → Letters and Mailings → Mail Merge Wizard; select the E-mail Messages option, click Next, and follow the steps in the wizard.

`02+` *Create and send form faxes using a list of recipients or my Outlook contact list?*
Tools → Letters and Mailings → Mail Merge Wizard; select the Faxes option, click Next, and follow the steps in the wizard. Note that this option is unavailable unless you have a MAPI-compatible fax program and email program with a fax transport installed.

Create a letter using a wizard?
Tools → Letters and Mailings → Letter Wizard (Tools → Letter Wizard in Word 97 and 2000).

Print an envelope?
Tools → Letters and Mailings → Envelopes and Labels. Enter a delivery address and return address, and click Print.

NOTE

In Word 97 and 2000, the Envelopes and Labels command is directly on the Tools menu.

> *Use addresses from an address book on an envelope?*
>
> Tools → Letters and Mailings → Envelopes and Labels; click the Insert Address button above the mailing address or return address to look up an address from your Windows Address Book.

Change the envelope size and other options?
Tools → Letters and Mailings → Envelopes and Labels → Options → Envelope Options.

Change how an envelope is printed?
Tools → Letters and Mailings → Envelopes and Labels → Options → Printing Options.

Print labels?
Tools → Letters and Mailings → Envelopes and Labels → Labels; enter the address, choose whether to print a single label or a sheet of the same labels, and click Print.

Use addresses from an address book for labels?
Tools → Letters and Mailings → Envelopes and Labels → Labels; use the Insert Address button to choose an address from the Windows Address Book.

Select a label type and change label details?
Tools → Letters and Mailings → Envelopes and Labels → Labels → Options.

Setting Other Word Options

The following tasks detail important options available through the Tools → Options command that are not discussed elsewhere in this part.

How do I...

Keep Word from repaginating documents in the background while I'm doing other things?
> Tools → Options → General → uncheck Background Repagination.

View my documents on a blue background with white text?
> Tools → Options → General → check Blue background, white text.

Use sounds and animated cursors to show what's going on in Word?
> Tools → Options → General; select the Provide Feedback with Sound and "Provide feedback with animation" options.

Have Word ask before performing a conversion when I open a document in a non-Word format?
> Tools → Options → General → Confirm conversion at Open.

Mail documents as attachments instead of in the email message body when using the File → Send To → Mail Recipient command?
> Tools → Options → General → Mail as Attachment.

Change the unit of measurement I use in rulers and dialog boxes?
> Tools → Options → General → Measurement Units.

🔳 *Set options for how Web pages are created and displayed?*
> Tools → Options → General → Web Options.

🔳 *Set email options for when I use the File → Send To → Mail Recipient command?*
> Tools → Options → General → E-Mail Options.

Change the name, initials, and address I use in Word?
    Tools → Options → User Information.

Pick the font used as a substitute when I am missing the actual font used in a document?
    Tools → Options → Compatibility → Font Substitution.

Getting Help

The following tasks cover the help options available in Word.

How do I...

Make the Office Assistant go away?
    Right-click the assistant's icon and choose Hide to temporarily remove the assistant. Right-click the icon and choose Options → Use the Office Assistant to turn it off entirely (in Word 97, you can't turn off the assistant with one click; you must disable each action it responds to).

View the tips suggested by the Office Assistant?
    As you work, a light bulb appears on the assistant when Word sees an easier way to do something you are doing. Click the assistant to see its suggestions.

Ask Word a question?
    Click the assistant and type a question. If the assistant is turned off, click the Ask a Question box on the menu bar and type a question.

Use the full help window?
    In Word 97 and 2000, use Help → Microsoft Word Help; browse the contents, click the Answer Wizard tab to search for topics, or click the Index tab to search for keywords.

    In Word 97, use Help → Contents and Index.

Get a description of a toolbar button or other screen element?
    In the main Word window, use Help → What's This? (or Shift-F1) and then click an interface element (to open a help balloon) or any text (to reveal formatting).

Get help if I'm used to using WordPerfect?
> Help → WordPerfect Help.

Have Word display the equivalent Word command when you press a WordPerfect key combination?
> Tools → Options → General → Help for WordPerfect Users.

Change the functions of Page Up, Page Down, Home, End, and Esc to their WordPerfect equivalents?
> Tools → Options → General → Navigation Keys for WordPerfect Users.

00+ *Have Office scan its program files and replace them from the original installation files if any problems are found?*
> Help → Detect and Repair. You'll need to provide the installation CD or the location of the installation files.

Customizing Word

The following tasks show you how to set options for and change the commands on Word's menus and toolbars. This section also shows you how to assign keyboard shortcuts to commands.

Setting General Customization Options

How do I...

00+ *Have Word show the full menus instead of only common commands?*
> Tools → Customize → Options → Always Show Full Menus.

00+ *Show the Standard toolbar and Formatting toolbar on two rows?*
> Tools → Customize → Options → Show Standard and Formatting Toolbars on Two Rows.

> You can also drag the Formatting toolbar to the second row and Word will automatically enable this option.

Use larger icons on toolbars?
>Tools → Customize → Options → Large icons.

00+ *Specify whether font names should be displayed using the actual font in the Font drop-down list?*
>Tools → Customize → Options → List Font Names in Their Font.

Turn off or on the pop-up balloon tips showing the names of toolbar buttons?
>Tools → Customize → Options → Show ScreenTips on toolbars.

Have Word show shortcut keys for toolbar buttons in pop-up balloon tips?
>Tools → Customize → Options → Show shortcut keys in ScreenTips.

Customizing Toolbars and Menus

How do I...

Turn on toolbars not shown in Word's View → Toolbars sub-menu?
>Tools → Customize → Toolbars; click the checkbox next to any toolbar to turn it on.

Create a new toolbar that I can fill with buttons and menus?
>Tools → Customize → Toolbars → New.

Rename a toolbar that I have created?
>Tools → Customize → Toolbars; select a toolbar and click Rename.

Restore a toolbar to its default settings?
>Tools → Customize → Toolbars; select a toolbar and click Reset. Choose whether to reset the toolbar in the open document or the attached template.

Add a command to a toolbar or menu?
>Tools → Customize → Command. Select a category and a command from that category. Click Description to view

a pop-up explanation of the command. Drag the command to any toolbar or menu.

Add a command to a shortcut menu?

Tools → Customize → Toolbars; enable the Shortcut Menus toolbar. Switch the Commands tab and drag a command to any of the available shortcut menus on the toolbar. The toolbar closes as soon as you close the Customize dialog. See Part 1 for more on shortcut menus.

Remove a command from a toolbar or menu?

Tools → Customize. Drag the command from the menu and when the icon displays an X, drop the command to remove it.

Without opening the Customize dialog, hold down the Alt key while dragging any command away from the toolbar (this does not work with commands on menus in Word 97, but does work with menus and buttons).

Change the name of a menu command or toolbar button?

Tools → Customize. Right-click a command or button and change the value of the Name box on the shortcut menu.

Change the icon used for a command or toolbar button?

Tools → Customize. Right-click a command or button and choose Change Button Image.

Change how text is displayed for a command or toolbar button?

Tools → Customize. Right-click a command or button and choose Default Style, Text Only (Always), Text Only (In Menus), or Text and Image.

Insert a dividing line between buttons on a toolbar or commands on a menu?

Tools → Customize. Right-click a command or button that will be to the right of (or below) the dividing line and choose Begin a Group.

Choose where to save changes made to toolbars and menus?

Tools → Customize → Commands → Save In. The file you specify will be used to save all changes you make while the Customize dialog is open.

Customizing Keyboard Shortcuts

How do I...

Find out the default keyboard shortcut for a command?

Tools → Customize → Keyboard; select a category and a command to see current assignments in the Current keys box. Refer to the tables in Part 3 for a list of default keyboard shortcuts.

Assign a keyboard shortcut to a command?

Tools → Customize → Keyboard; select a category and a command. Click in the "Press new shortcut key" box and then press the key combination you want to use. Choose where to save the changes and click Assign.

Assign a shortcut key to a symbol, special character, font, AutoText entry, macro, or style?

Tools → Customize → Keyboard. Use the special categories at the bottom of the category list.

Print a list of shortcut keys used in a document or template?

Tools → Macro → Macros. In the Macros In box, select Word Commands. In the Macro Name box, select ListCommands. Click Run. In the List Commands dialog that appears, select Current menu and keyboard settings and click OK. A table of shortcut keys is created in the document window.

Collaborating

The following tasks describe the collaboration tools provided by Word, including the ability to send and route documents, track changes to a document, insert comments, and compare documents.

Sending Documents to People and Places

How do I...

Send a document by email, making the document the body of the message?
> File → Send To → Mail Recipient.

00+ *Send a document by email as an attachment?*
> File → Send To → Mail Recipient (as Attachment).

02+ *Send a document as an attachment for review?*
> File → Send To → Mail Recipient (as Review) to send the document as an attachment and flag the recipient that the document is to be reviewed.

00+ *Send a document to a folder on an Exchange server or a folder in my Outlook personal folder store?*
> File → Send To → Exchange Folder.

Route a document by email so that multiple people can review it?
> File → Send To → Routing Recipient. You can designate the route through the recipients the document will take and monitor its progress.

Set compatibility features for users of other versions of Word?
> Tools → Options → Compatibility. Use the drop-down list to choose a program. Default compatibility features for the program are chosen and you can use the list to further customize.

Set a password required to open or modify the document?
> Tools → Options → Security (Tools → Options → Save in Word 97 and 2000). If you forget a password, you'll need to find a third party utility that can crack it. Check out *http://www.elcomsoft.com/* for one such program.

00+ *Start a meeting with someone using NetMeeting and open the current document for review?*
> Tools → Online Collaboration → Meet Now.

Comments

How do I...

View or hide comments and other markup in a document?

In Word 2002, View → Markup toggles whether markup (including comments and tracked changes) is shown at all. In Print Layout View, comments and changes are shown in balloons in the right margin. Use the Show button on the Reviewing toolbar to specify the kinds of markup that are shown. Show → Comments toggles whether comments are shown. In Normal View, you must use the Reviewing Pane button on the Reviewing toolbar to view comments, although you can use this pane in Print Layout View if you want.

In Word 97 and 2000, View → Comments toggles whether the Comments pane is shown at the bottom of the screen. Markup balloons are not used in these versions.

Insert a new comment?

Place the insertion point or make a selection and use Insert → Comment.

Change a comment?

In Word 2002, click the text of a comment in the balloon or Reviewing Pane to edit it.

In Word 97 and 2000, use View → Comments and then click the text of the comment in the Comment pane to edit it.

Delete a comment?

Right-click the comment in the main text, the comment bubble (Word 2002 only), or the Reviewing Pane and select Delete Comment.

In Word 2002, you can also select the change and click the Reject Change/Delete Comment button on the Reviewing toolbar.

Delete all comments in a document?

> On the Reviewing toolbar, click the down arrow next to the Reject Change/Delete Comment button and choose Reject All Comments in Document.

Change the format used for comment text in comment bubbles?

> Click the text in a comment bubble (the Reviewing Pane does not work). Select Format → Styles and Formatting. Right-click the Comment Text style and choose Modify.

Tracking Changes

How do I...

Hide or show all tracked changes in a document?

> In Word 2002, use View → Markup.
>
> In Word 97 and 2000, use Tools → Track Changes → Highlight Changes.

Have Word track the changes to a document?

Tools → Track Changes, Ctrl-Shift-E, or double-click the TRK text on the status bar. Each of these toggles tracked changes on or off. If tracking is enabled, all edits to a document appear in a new color for each author and underlined, by default.

Choose the specific markup types to display?

> On the Reviewing toolbar, use the options on the Show menu to hide or show specific types of changes or changes by specific reviewers.

Change how tracked changes are displayed?

> On the Reviewing toolbar, make a selection on the Display for Review drop-down list.
>
> In Word 97 and 2000, use Tools → Track Changes → Highlight Changes.

Move between changes in a document?

> On the Reviewing toolbar, click Previous or Next.

Make a change permanent by accepting it?

On the Reviewing toolbar, click the Accept Change button.

Right-click a change in the document window and choose Accept *change* (the command changes depending on the type of change).

You can also select a range of text and accept all the comments in it using the Accept Change button.

Accept all changes in a document?

In Word 2002, on the Reviewing toolbar, click the down arrow next to the Accept Change button and choose Accept All Changes in Document.

In Word 97 and 2000, use use Tools → Track Changes → Accept or Reject Changes → Accept All.

Undo a change by rejecting it?

On the Reviewing toolbar, click Reject Change/Delete Comment.

Right-click a change in the document window and choose Reject *change* (the command changes depending on the type of change).

Select a range of text and click the Reject Change/Delete Comment button to reject all changes in the text.

Reject all changes in a document?

In Word 2002, on the Reviewing toolbar, click the down arrow next to the Reject Change/Delete Comment button and choose Reject All Changes in Document.

In Word 97 and 2000, use Tools → Track Changes → Accept or Reject Changes → Reject All.

Change basic options for tracking changes?

In Word 2002, use Tools → Options → Track Changes or click the Show → Options command on the Reviewing toolbar.

In Word 97 and 2000, use Tools → Track Changes → Highlight Changes → Options.

In all versions, right-click the TRK text in the status bar and select Options.

02+ *Change whether markup balloons are used in Print and Web Layout views?*

Tools → Options → Track Changes → Use Balloons in Print and Web Layout.

02+ *Change the size and placement of markup balloons?*

Tools → Options → Track Changes; use the options in the Balloons section of the dialog.

Change how Word uses change lines to indicate where markup has occurred?

In Word 2002, use Tools → Options → Track Changes; use options in the Changed Lines section.

In Word 97 and 2000, use Tools → Options → Highlight Changes → Options.

> **Print the markup in a document?**
> File → Print; use the Print What drop-down list to choose either "Document showing markup" or "List of markup."

Protect the changes or comments in a document when sending it for review?

Tools → Protect Document → Tracked Changes to prevent a user from turning off tracked changes and from accepting or rejecting changes. Specify a password to prevent other users from being able to go in and remove protection via the same method.

Comparing Documents

How do I...

Compare two documents by merging them and viewing the differences as tracked changes?

In Word 2002, open one document (preferably an edited copy). Select Tools → Compare and Merge Documents.

Select the second document (preferably the original copy), and then choose one of the following options:

- To display results as marked changes in the second document (the original), click Merge.
- To display results as marked changes in the first document (the copy), choose Merge into Current Document.
- To display results as marked changes in a new document, choose Merge into New Document.

    In Word 97 and 2000, open one document and then use the Tools → Merge Documents command to select another document to merge into the first.

Use the Compare and Merge feature on more than two documents?

You can repeat the Tools → Compare and Merge (or Tools → Merge Documents) process on multiple documents until they are all combined in a single document. This may be okay for bringing in small changes from multiple reviewers who each had their own copy, but it's usually easier to merge two documents at a time, go through the changes, and then bring in additional documents one at a time.

02+ *Compare document using a legal black line instead of tracked changes?*

Open the first document, choose Tools → Compare and Merge Documents, select the Legal Blackline option, select the second document, and click Compare. A third document is created, showing only what changed between the two documents.

00+ *Use web discussions for a document?*

Tools → Online Collaborations → Web Discussions. Web discussions are shown in a separate pane at the bottom of the document and a Web Discussions toolbar opens with options for creating, replying to, filtering, and printing discussions. This feature requires that a discussion server be set up and configured on your network.

The first time you use the feature, you may be prompted to select a discussion server.

Using Macros

The following tips describe the basics of using macros in Word. Macros allow you to perform a set of tasks or steps in Word all at once.

How do I...

Set a security level for enabling macros?
For Word 2000 and 2002, use Tools → Macro → Security → Security Level.

For Word 97, use Tools → Options → General → Macro virus protection. Enalbing this option forces Word to prompt you when opening a document with macros.

00+ *View trusted sources for macros?*
Tools → Macro → Security → Trusted Sources.

Record a new macro?

Tools → Macro → Record New Macro. Name the macro, choose where to assign and save it, click OK, and then perform the actions you want to record. Use the record, pause, and stop buttons on the Stop Recording toolbar to control the recording.

Launch Visual Basic for Applications to create or edit a macro?
Tools → Macro → Visual Basic Editor (or Alt-F11).

Run a macro?
Tools → Macro → Macros (or Alt-F8).

Run a macro one step at a time, showing me each step in VBA as it occurs in Word?
Tools → Macro → Macros; select the macro and click Step Into.

Delete a macro?

Tools → Macro → Macros; select the macro and click Delete.

Copy macros to another document or template?

Tools → Macro → Macros → Organizer.

Tools → Templates and Add-Ins → Organizer → Macro Project Items.

PART III

Word Reference

This part of the book provides reference information that is otherwise difficult to find.

- Useful commands that are not included on any toolbar or menu by default (Table 1)
- Text and graphic file formats that Word natively supports (Table 2 and Table 3)
- Switches to start Word from the command line (Table 4)
- Wildcards and character codes for search-and-replace operations (Table 5 and Table 6)
- Locations of important Word files and default paths for saving files (Table 7)

In addition, this part lists default key combinations (keyboard shortcuts) for:

- Selecting, formatting, and editing text (Tables 8–14)
- Inserting and reviewing text (Table 15 and Table 16)
- Performing a mail merge (Table 17)
- Printing and previewing (Table 18)
- Fields (Table 19)
- Outlines (Table 20)
- Command bars (Table 21)
- Windows and dialog boxes (Table 22)
- The Web (Table 23)
- Cross-references and footnotes (Table 24)
- Office Assistant keys (Table 25)

Don't forget that you can assign your own keyboard short-cuts for many of these and other Word operations via Tools → Customize → Keyboard.

Command Reference

There are over 1000 commands available in Word 2002 and only some of them made their way onto Word's menus and toolbars or were given keyboard shortcuts. Table 1 lists some useful commands and suggestions on where you might add them. Check out the section on customizing Word in Part 2 for details on adding these commands to the interface.

Table 1. Useful Word commands

Command	Action	Suggested Uses
ResetChar	Removes all character formatting, reverting text to the default paragraph formatting. Same as pressing Ctrl-Space or choosing Clear Formatting from Style drop-down list.	Add button to formatting toolbar, macro, or to Text shortcut menu.
Hidden	Applies the Hidden format to selected text, same as Format → Font → Hidden.	Add to shortcut menu or toolbar for hiding text within a document. See Part 2 for more.
NextMisspelling	Jumps to the next misspelled word, selects it, and opens a shortcut menu.	Add to a toolbar to quickly browse through misspelled words in a document.
AutoScroll	Automatically scrolls the document in the direction that you move the mouse. Some three-button mice do this when you click the middle button.	Add to a toolbar for an easy way to scan through long documents.
ApplyHeadingX	Three commands (ApplyHeading1–3) apply the default heading paragraph styles. Same as Alt-Ctrl-*x* (where *x* is the heading number).	Add to the Text shortcut menu to quickly make headings throughout a document.

Table 1. Useful Word commands (continued)

Command	Action	Suggested Uses
EditSwapAllNotes	Changes all footnotes in a document to endnotes and vice versa.	Add to a toolbar for quick conversion without having to select and convert individual notes.
EndOfWindowExtend	Extend the current selection (or create a new selection from the insertion point) through the last line fully displayed in the document window.	Add to a toolbar or shortcut menu to extend your selection capabilities.
MenuWork	A new menu that works like a favorites menu for frequently-used documents.	Add to Word's menu bar.
SentLeft (SentRight)	Moves the insertion point to the beginning of the previous (sentleft) or next (sentright) sentence.	Add to toolbar or create a keyboard shortcut for browsing sentences.
SentLeftExtend (SentRightExtend)	Extends the selection to include the previous or next sentence.	Add to toolbar or shortcut menu or create a keyboard shortcut.
SkipNumbering	Removes numbering or bullets from the selected paragraphs and continues the numbering or bulleting for subsequent items.	Add to toolbar or Lists shortcut menu.
TableSelectTable	Selects an entire table. Pressing Alt-5 (using the 5 on the number pad) while NumLock is turned off also selects a table.	Add to Table Cell, Table Text, and Table Lists shortcut menus.
ToolsCustomizeKey-Board	Opens the Customize Keyboard dialog (Tools → Customize → Keyboard).	Add to a toolbar for quick access.
ToolsCustomizeKey-BoardShortcut	Changes the pointer to a command button. Clicking any toolbar button or menu command opens the Customize Keyboard dialog with that command selected.	Add to a toolbar to quickly customize any command.

Table 1. *Useful Word commands (continued)*

Command	Action	Suggested Uses
ToolsSpellingHide	Hides/shows the squiggly red lines under misspelled words.	Add to toolbar for quick access.
ToolsGrammarHide	Hides/shows the squiggly green lines under grammatical errors.	Add to toolbar.

Native Formats

Word 2002 supports many text and graphic formats without the need to convert them. Table 2 lists all of the text formats that are native to Word 2002 and need no conversion. Table 3 shows the native graphics formats. Note that other text and graphics formats can be used in Word if the correct filters are installed, some of which are included with the Word installation files.

Table 2. *Native text formats*

Format	File Extension
Word 2002, Word 2000, and Word 97 for Windows	*.doc*
Word 98 for the Macintosh	*.doc*
HTML	*.htm and .html*
MS-DOS Text	*.txt*
MS-DOS Text with Line Breaks	*.txt*
Rich Text Format	*.rtf*
Text Only	*.txt*
Text with Line Breaks	*.txt*
Unicode Text	*.txt*
Word 6.0/95 for Windows and Macintosh	*.doc*
Word 4.x– 5.1 for Macintosh (import only)	*.mcw*
Word 2.0 and 1.0 for Windows (import only)	*.doc*

Table 3. Native graphic formats

Format	File Extension	Versions	Notes
Graphics Interchange Format	.gif	Native in Word 2000, 2002. Word 97 imports using HTML converter.	Supports versions GIF87a (including interlacing) and GIF89a (including interlacing and transparency).
Joint Photographic Experts Group	.jpg .jpeg	Native in all versions.	Supports version 6.0 of the JPEG File Interchange Format (JFIF).
Portable Network Graphics	.png	Native in all versions.	Supports files conforming to the Tenth Specification Version 1.0.
Windows bitmap	.bmp	Native in all versions.	Supports Windows and OS/2 bitmaps, Run Length Encoded (RLE) bitmaps, and device-independent bitmaps (DIB).
Tagged Image File Format	.tiff	Native in Word 2000, 2002. Word 97 converts on opening.	Supports TIFF Specification Revision 5.0 and 6.0, Part1: Baseline TIFF.
Windows Enhanced Metafile	.emf	Native in all versions.	
Windows Metafile	.wmf	Native in all versions.	

Startup Switches

Like most programs, you can start Word from the Windows command line (Start → Programs → MS-DOS Prompt in Windows 95/98/Me and Start → Programs → Accessories → Command Prompt in Windows 2000/XP) or when creating customized shortcuts for starting Word. At the prompt, type winword.exe to launch Word normally, or add one of the switches listed in Table 4 after the command to affect how Word launches (for instance, winword.exe /n).

Table 4. Command-line startup switches

Startup Switch	Description
filename	Starts Word and opens the specified file. You can specify more than one filename (separated by spaces) to open multiple documents.
/a	Starts Word and prevents and add-ins and global templates from loading. The switch also locks the setting files, so that no settings may be modified when Word is started with this switch.
/l *addinpath*	Starts Word normally and loads a specific add in or global template. For example, `winword.exe /l c:\word\newglobal.dot` loads a template named *newglobal.dot* found in the *C:\word* folder.
/m	Starts Word without running any AutoExec macros, which are macros set to run when Word starts or a particular document opens. You can also do this by holding down the Shift key while starting Word normally.
/m *macroname*	Starts Word without running any AutoExec macros and has Word run the specified macro on starting.
/n	Starts a new instance of Word with no document open. Documents opened in each instance of Word will not appear as choices in the Window menu of other instances.
/t *template_name*	Starts Word with a new document based on a template other than *Normal.dot*.
/w	Starts a new instance of Word with a blank document. Documents opened in each instance of Word will not appear as choices in the Window menu of the other instances.
/regserver	Forces Word to rewrite all of its registry keys and reassociate itself with Word files, then exits Word. Use if you are having a problem with file type associations.
/unregserver	Removes file type registrations from the Windows Registry and the Registered file types list (in Windows Explorer).

Wildcards and Find Codes

You can do sophisticated searches using the Edit → Find and Edit → Replace commands in combination with wildcards and special character codes. In order to use wildcards, you must have the Use Wildcards option turned on (Edit → Find → More → Use Wildcards or Edit → Replace → More → Use Wildcards). However, many of the special character codes work differently when the Use Wildcards option is turned on or off.

Wildcards are listed in Table 5 and special character codes are listed in Table 6.

NOTE

In the world outside Word, the expressions that Word refers to as *wildcards* are known as *regular expressions*, and are a syntax for handling text. Technically, wildcards are only a subset of regular expressions (such as the ? and * symbols), though Microsoft has decided to refer to them all as wildcards in Word. They work a little differently (as do most implementations of regular expressions), but achieve much the same effect. See *Word Power Tools* by Westley Annis (O'Reilly & Associates, 2003) for more information on using wildcards and regular expressions in Word.

Table 5. Wildcards used in Edit → Find and Edit → Replace

Name	Symbol	Example
Any character	?	"a?t" finds "act" and "art"
Specified characters	[ ]	"[fp]act" finds "fact" and "pact"
Any character in range	[-]	"[a-o]act" finds "fact" but not "pact"
Any character not in range	[!-]	"[!a-o]act" finds "pact" but not "fact"
Beginning of word	<	"<act" finds "act" and "action"
End of word	>	">act" finds "react" and "fact"
Not	[!]	"[!p]act" finds "act" and "fact" but not "pact"
0 or more characters	*	"*act>" finds all words where "act" are the last three letters.
Exactly *n* occurrences of a character	{n}	"re{2}d" finds all occurrences of "reed" but not "red"

Table 5. *Wildcards used in Edit → Find and Edit →*
Replace (continued)

Name	Symbol	Example
At least *n* occurrences of a character	{n,}	"re{1,}d" finds all occurences of "reed" and "reed"
Between *n* and *m* occurences of a character	{n,m}	"15{1-3}" finds "150", "1500", and "15000"
One or more occurences of the previous character	@	"re@d" finds "red" and "reed"

Table 6. *Character codes used in Edit → Find and Edit →*
Replace

Special Character	Symbol	Notes
Paragraph mark	^p	Cannot be used in the Find what box when wildcard search is enabled. With Wildcards on, use ^13 in the Find what box instead.
Tab	^t	
ANSI or ASCII characters	^0nnn	*nnn* represents the character code.
Em dash	^+	—
En dash	^=	-
Caret character	^^	
Manual line break	^l	
Column break	^n	
Manual page break	^m	This code searches for section breaks when wildcards are turned on.
Nonbreaking space	^s	
Nonbreaking hyphen	^~	
Optional hyphen	^-	
Graphic	^g	Works only with Find (not replace) and only when wildcards are on.
Any character	^?	Works only with Find and when wildcards are off.
Any digit	^#	Works only with Find and when wildcards are off.

Table 6. Character codes used in Edit → Find and Edit →
Replace (continued)

Special Character	Symbol	Notes
Any letter	^$	Works only with Find and when wildcards are off.
Footnote mark	^f	Works only with Find and when wildcards are off. With wildcards on, use ^2 instead.
Endnote mark	^e	Works only with Find and when wildcards are off. With wildcards on, use ^2 instead.
Field	^d	Works only with Find and when wildcards are off. With wildcards on, use ^19 instead.
Section break	^b	Works only with Find and when wildcards are off.
White space (regular and nonbreaking spaces and tabs)	^w	Works only with Find and when wildcards are off.
Windows Clipboard contents	^c	Works only with Replace (not Find).
Contents of the Find what box	^&	Works only with Replace (not Find).

Default File Locations

Table 7 lists the locations of important files and folders for Word 2002. Some of these locations are user-definable; some are not.

Table 7. Default file locations

File or Location	Operating System	Path	User-Definable
Document storage	Windows 95/98/Me	*C:\My Documents*	Yes
	Windows 2000/XP	*C:\Documents and Settings\<username>\ My Documents*	Yes
User Templates (including *Normal. dot*)	Word 2000 and 2002 in Windows 95/98/ Me	*C:\Windows\Application Data\Microsoft\ Templates*	Yes

Table 7. Default file locations (continued)

File or Location	Operating System	Path	User-Definable
	Word 2000 and 2002 in Windows 2000/XP	*C:\Documents and Settings\\<username>\ Application Data\ Microsoft\Templates*	Yes
	Word 97 in all versions of Windows	*C:\Program Files\ Microsoft Office\ Templates*	Yes
Workgroup Templates		No default directory. Set using Tools → Options → File Locations	Yes
AutoRecover Files	Windows 95/98/Me	*C:\Windows\Application Data\Microsoft\Word*	Yes
	Windows 2000/XP	*C:\Documents and Settings\username\ Application Data\ Microsoft\Word*	Yes
Startup directory for additional templates or add-ins	Word 2000 and 2002 in Windows 95/98/ Me	*C:\Windows\Application Data\Microsoft\Word\ Startup*	Yes
	Word 2000 and 2002 in Windows 2000/XP	*C:\Documents and Settings\\<username>\ Application Data\ Microsoft\Word\Startup*	Yes
	Word 97 in all versions of Windows	*C:\Program Files\ Microsoft Office\Office\ Startup*	Yes
Built-in templates and wizards (English-language installation)	Windows	*C:\Program Files\ Microsoft Office\ Templates\1033*	No
Program Files	Word 2002 in all versions of Windows	*C:\Program Files\ Microsoft Office\Office10*	No
	Word 97 and 2000 in all versions of Windows	*C:\Program Files\ Microsoft Office\Office*	No

Table 7. Default file locations (continued)

File or Location	Operating System	Path	User-Definable
Startup folder for all users	Windows	C:\Program Files\ Microsoft Office\ Office10\Startup	No
History of recently opened documents	Windows 95/98/Me	C:\Windows\Application Data\Microsoft\Office\ Recent	No
	Windows 2000/XP	C:\Documents and Settings\<username>\ Application Data\ Microsoft\Office\Recent	No

Keyboard Shortcuts

Word supports hundreds of built-in key combinations. Don't be overwhelmed, though. Find the few that represent frequent tasks and start with those.

NOTE

Word also allows you to assign your own key combinations, as described in Part 2, *Word Tasks*. Key combinations you assign override any built-in combinations they may conflict with.

The following tables of default key combinations (Tables 8–25) are grouped by function. Each focuses on a certain topic in Word, such as selecting text, applying character formatting, or working with tables. Unless otherwise noted, these shortcuts work the same in Word 97, 2000, and 2002.

Table 8. General program keys

Key	Action
Ctrl-N	Create a new document
Ctrl-O or Ctrl-F12	Open a document

Table 8. General program keys (continued)

Key	Action
Ctrl-S or Shift-F12	Save a document
F12	Open the Save As dialog
Ctrl-W or Alt-F4	Close a document. If it is the only document open, this action exits Word.
Ctrl-Z	Undo an action
Ctrl-Y or F4	Redo or repeat an action
Alt-Ctrl-S	Split a document or remove a split view
Alt-Ctrl-P	Switch to page layout view
Alt-Ctrl-O	Switch to outline view
Alt-Ctrl-N	Switch to normal view
Ctrl-\	Move between a master document and its subdocuments
F1	Open Help or Office Assistant
Shift-F1	Context-sensitive help or reveal formatting (as with Help → What's This?)
Ctrl-F6	Go to the next Window
Ctrl-Shift-F6	Go to the previous window
F7	Run the Spelling and Grammar checker
Shift-F7	Open the thesaurus
F10	Activate the Menu bar
Shift-F10 or the context button on some keyboards	Open a context menu

Table 9. Movement keys

Key	Action
Left	Move the insertion point one character to the left
Right	Move one character to the right
Ctrl-Left	Move one word to the left

Table 9. Movement keys (continued)

Key	Action
Ctrl-Right	Move one word to the right
Ctrl-Up	Move one paragraph up
Ctrl-Down	Move one paragraph down
Up	Move up one line
Down	Move down one line
End	Move to the end of a line
Home	Move to the beginning of a line
Alt-Ctrl-Page Up	Move to the top of the window
Alt-Ctrl-Page Down	Move to the end of the window
Page Up	Move up one screen
Page Down	Move down one screen
Ctrl-Page Up	Move to the previous browse object
Ctrl-Page Down	Move to the next browse object
Ctrl-Home	Move to the beginning of a document
Ctrl-End	Move to the end of a document
Shift-F5	Move back up to three previous revisions or to the location of the insertion point when the document was last closed

Table 10. Selection keys

Key	Action
Shift-Right	Extend selection one character to the right
Shift-Left	Extend selection one character to the left
Ctrl-Shift-Right	Extend selection to the end of the next word
Ctrl-Shift-Left	Extend selection to the beginning of the previous word
Shift-End	Extend selection to the end of a line
Shift-Home	Extend selection to the beginning of a line
Shift-Down	Extend selection one line down
Shift-Up	Extend selection one line up
Ctrl-Shift-Down	Extend selection to the end of a paragraph

Table 10. Selection keys (continued)

Key	Action
Ctrl-Shift-Up	Extend selection to the beginning of a paragraph
Shift-Page Down	Extend selection one screen down
Shift-Page Up	Extend selection one screen up
Alt-Ctrl-Page Down	Extend selection to the end of a window
Ctrl-Shift-Home	Extend selection to the beginning of a document
Ctrl-A	Select the entire document
F8	Enter extend selection mode. Use arrows to extend selection. Press F8 repeatedly to extend a selection as follows: first press enters mode, second selects word next to insertion point, third selects the whole sentence, fourth selects all characters in paragraph (including the paragraph mark), fifth adds the whole document. Use ESC to exit extend mode.
Shift-F8	Reduce the size of a selection while in extend selection mode
Ctrl-Shift-F8-arrow keys	Extend selection to a vertical block of text
F8-arrow keys	Extend selection to a specific location in a document

Table 11. Character formatting keys

Key	Action
Ctrl-Shift-F	Activate the Font drop-down menu on the Formatting toolbar
Ctrl-Shift-P	Activate the Font Size drop-down menu on the Formatting toolbar
Ctrl-Shift →	Increase the font size according to the preset sizes
Ctrl-Shift-<	Decrease the font size according to the preset sizes
Ctrl-]	Increase the font size by 1 point
Ctrl-[	Decrease the font size by 1 point
Ctrl-D	Open the Format → Font dialog
Shift-F3	Cycle through the available case formats for letters
Ctrl-Shift-A	Format letters as all capitals
Ctrl-Shift-K	Format letters as small capitals
Ctrl-B	Apply bold formatting
Ctrl-I	Apply italic formatting

Table 11. Character formatting keys (continued)

Key	Action
Ctrl-U	Apply underline formatting
Ctrl-Shift-W	Underline words but not spaces
Ctrl-Shift-D	Double-underline text
Ctrl-Shift-H	Apply hidden text formatting
Ctrl-= (equal)	Apply subscript formatting (automatic spacing)
Ctrl-Shift-Plus	Apply superscript formatting (automatic spacing)
Ctrl-Shift-Q	Change the selection to Symbol font
Ctrl-Shift-*	Display non-printing characters
Ctrl-Shift-C	Copy formats
Ctrl-Shift-V	Paste formats
Shift-F1-any text	Review text formatting (same as Help → What's This?)
Ctrl-Space	Remove manual character formatting

Table 12. Paragraph formatting keys

Key	Action
Ctrl-1	Single-space lines
Ctrl-2	Double-space lines
Ctrl-5	Set 1.5-line spacing
Ctrl-0 (zero)	Add/Remove one-line spacing preceding a paragraph
Ctrl-E	Center a paragraph
Ctrl-J	Justify a paragraph
Ctrl-L	Left-align a paragraph
Ctrl-R	Right-align a paragraph
Ctrl-M	Indent a paragraph from the left
Ctrl-Shift-M	Remove a paragraph indent from the left
Ctrl-T	Create a hanging indent
Ctrl-Shift-T	Reduce a hanging indent
Ctrl-Shift-S	Activate the Style drop-down list on the Formatting toolbar
Alt-Ctrl-K	Start AutoFormat
Ctrl-Shift-N	Apply the Normal style

Table 12. Paragraph formatting keys (continued)

Key	Action
Alt-Ctrl-1	Apply the Heading 1 style
Alt-Ctrl-2	Apply the Heading 2 style
Alt-Ctrl-3	Apply the Heading 3 style
Ctrl-Shift-L	Apply the List style
Ctrl-Q	Remove paragraph formatting

Table 13. Editing keys

Key	Action
Backspace	Delete one character to the left
Ctrl-Backspace	Delete one word to the left
Delete	Delete one character to the right
Ctrl-Delete	Delete one word to the right
Ctrl-X or Shift-Delete	Cut selected text or graphics to the Clipboard
Ctrl-F3	Cut selected text to the Spike
Ctrl-C or Ctrl-Insert	Copy text or graphics to the Clipboard
Ctrl-V or Shift-Insert	Paste the Clipboard contents
Ctrl-Shift-F3	Paste the Spike contents
Ctrl-C, Ctrl-C	Display the Clipboard
F2	Move text or graphics (move insertion point after pressing F2 and press Enter to place selection)
Alt-F3	Create AutoText
Alt-Shift-R	Copy the header or footer used in the previous section of the document

Table 14. Insertion keys

Key	Action
Ctrl-F9	Insert an empty field
Shift-Enter	Insert a line break
Ctrl-Enter	Insert a page break

Table 14. Insertion keys (continued)

Key	Action
Ctrl-Shift-Enter	Insert a column break
Ctrl-Hyphen	Insert an optional hyphen
Ctrl-Shift-Hyphen	Insert a non-breaking hyphen
Ctrl-Shift-Space	Insert a non-breaking space
Alt-Ctrl-C	Insert a copyright symbol
Alt-Ctrl-R	Insert a registered trademark symbol
Alt-Ctrl-T	Insert a trademark symbol
Alt-Ctrl-Period	Insert an ellipsis
Alt-Ctrl-E	In Word 2000 and 2002, insert a Euro symbol. In Word 97, this shortcut opens the endnote pane.

Table 15. Table keys

Key	Action
Tab	Move to the next cell in a row and select its contents, if any
Shift-Tab	Move to and select the previous cell in a row
Alt-Home	Move to the first cell in a row
Alt-End	Move to the last cell in a row
Alt-Page Up	Move to the first cell in a column
Alt-Page Down	Move to the last cell in a column
Up	Move to the previous row
Down	Move to the next row
Shift-Up	Select the cell in the previous row. Continue pressing the arrow key while the Shift key is depressed to add more rows to the selection.
Alt-5 (with Num Lock off)	Select an entire table

Table 16. Reviewing keys

Key	Action
Alt-Ctrl-M	Insert a comment
Ctrl-Shift-E	Turn revision marks on or off

Table 16. Reviewing keys (continued)

Key	Action
Ctrl-Home	Go to the beginning of a comment
Ctrl-End	Go to the end of a comment

Table 17. Mail merge keys

Key	Action
Alt-Shift-K	Preview a mail merge
Alt-Shift-N	Merge a document
Alt-Shift-M	Print the merged document
Alt-Shift-E	Edit a mail-merge data document
Alt-Shift-F	Insert a merge field

Table 18. Printing and previewing keys

Key	Action
Ctrl-P	Print a document
Alt-Ctrl-I	Switch to Print Preview
arrow keys	Move around the preview page when zoomed in
Page Up or Page Down	Move by one preview page when zoomed out
Ctrl-Home	Move to the first preview page when zoomed out
Ctrl-End	Move to the last preview page when zoomed out

Table 19. Field keys

Key	Action
Alt-Shift-D	Insert a DATE field
Alt-Shift-P	Insert a PAGE field
Alt-Shift-T	Insert a TIME field
Alt-Ctrl-L	In Word 97, insert a LISTNUM field. In Word 2000 and 2002, Alt-Ctrl-L starts a numbered list.
Ctrl-F9	Insert an empty field and move the insertion point inside it
F9	Update selected fields
Shift-F9	Toggle display of field codes for whole document

Table 19. Field keys (continued)

Key	Action
Ctrl-Shift-F9	Unlink a field
F11	Go to next field
Shift-F11	Go to previous field
Ctrl-F11	Lock selected field
Ctrl-Shift-F11	Unlock selected field

Table 20. Outlining keys

Key	Action
Alt-Shift-Left	Promote a paragraph
Alt-Shift-Right	Demote a paragraph
Ctrl-Shift-N	Demote a heading to body text
Alt-Shift-Up	Move selected paragraphs up
Alt-Shift-Down	Move selected paragraphs down
Alt-Shift-Plus	Expand text under a heading
Alt-Shift-Minus	Collapse text under a heading
Alt-Shift-A or the asterisk (*) key on the numeric keypad	Expand or collapse all text or headings
Slash (/) key on the numeric keypad	Hide or display character formatting
Alt-Shift-L	Show the first line of body text or all body text
Alt-Shift-1	Show all headings with the Heading 1 style
Alt-Shift-n	Show all headings up to Heading n

Table 21. Command bar keys

Key	Action
Shift-F10	Open a context menu
F10 or Alt	Make the menu bar active or close an active menu. Once the menu bar is active, you press the underlined letter of a menu or command to activate it.

Table 21. Command bar keys (continued)

Key	Action
Ctrl-Tab	Move to the next toolbar or menu bar
Ctrl-Shift-Tab	Move to the previous toolbar or menu bar
arrow keys	Move between commands on an active menu bar
Enter	Activate a selected command
Home	Select the first command on an active menu or submenu
End	Select the last command on an active menu or submenu
Esc	Close a visible menu or submenu, leaving the menu bar active
Ctrl-Alt-Hyphen	Pointer turns to minus sign. Open menu and click a command to remove from the menu.

Table 22. Common Windows and dialog box keys

Key	Action
Alt-Tab	Switch to the next program
Alt-Shift-Tab	Switch to the previous program
Ctrl-Esc or Windows logo key	Show the Windows Start menu
Ctrl-W	Close the active document window
Ctrl-F10	Maximize the document window
Ctrl-F5	Restore the active document window
Ctrl-F6	Switch to the next document window
Ctrl-Shift-F6	Switch to the previous document window
Alt-I	Open the folder list in the Open or Save As dialog box. Use the up and down arrow keys to select a folder from the list.
Alt-0 (zero)	Move the focus to the file list. Use the up and down arrows to select a file.
Alt-O or Enter	Open the selected file, same as clicking Open
Alt-n	Choose a toolbar button in the Open or Save As dialog box. Numbering of buttons begins on the left.
F5	Update (refresh) the files visible in the Open or Save As dialog box
Ctrl-Tab or Ctrl-Page Down	Switch to the next tab in a dialog box

Table 22. Common Windows and dialog box keys (continued)

Key	Action
Ctrl-Shift-Tab or Ctrl-Page Up	Switch to the previous tab in a dialog box
Tab	Move to the next option on a dialog box
Shift-Tab	Move to the previous option on a dialog box
arrow keys	Move between options in a selected drop-down list
Space	Toggle a selected option
Alt-letter key	Toggle an option using the underlined letter in its description
Esc	Cancel a dialog. When a drop-down list is open, ESC closes the list instead.
Enter	Close a dialog box, accepting the default action suggested or any settings made
Alt-Space	Open the System menu (with window commands like minimize, maximize, etc.). This is the same as right-clicking a window's taskbar button.

Table 23. Web keys

Key	Action
Ctrl-K	Insert a hyperlink
Alt-Left	Go back one page (if available)
Alt-Right	Go forward one page (if available)

Table 24. Cross-reference and footnote keys

Key	Action
Alt-Shift-O	Mark a table of contents entry
Alt-Shift-I	Mark a table of authorities entry
Alt-Shift-X	Mark an index entry
Alt-Ctrl-F	Insert a footnote
Alt-Ctrl-D	Insert an endnote

Table 25. Office Assistant keys

Key	Action
F1	Get Help from the Office Assistant
Alt-F6	In Word 2000 and 2002, make the Office Assistant balloon active. In Word 97, Alt-F6 and Ctrl-F6 both cycle between open windows.
Alt-n	Select from the topics the Office Assistant displays
Alt-Down	See more topics
Alt-Up	See previous topics
Esc	Close an Office Assistant message or a tip window
Alt-N	Display the next tip in a tip window
Alt-B	Display the previous tip in a tip window

PART IV

Word Resources

This part lists additional Word resources, including Internet sites, books, and Word utilities.

Internet Sites

Microsoft's Official Word Site
Official news and articles with tips and tricks.

http://www.microsoft.com/word

Office Update
Microsoft's update site for all versions of Office. It includes service packs and patches, and a download center with updates, add-ins, and more.

http://officeupdate.microsoft.com

Microsoft TechNet
Valuable technical articles and resources on all Microsoft products, as well as access to a knowledgebase with thousands of how-to and tech support articles on Word.

http://www.microsoft.com/technet/

Woody's Watch
Woody Leonhard's advice, news, and newsletters on all Microsoft Office products, including Word.

http://www.woodyswatch.com/

WordFAQ
A site with tips, techniques, and how-tos on Word.

http://www.wordfaq.com/

Word's Most Valued Professional (MVP) Site
> Home of the members of Microsoft's Most Valuable Professional (MVP) group for Word. Members are selected because of their contributions to the Word newsgroups (described next).

> *http://www.mvps.org/word*

Word newsgroups
> Microsoft maintains a news server that you can access using any newsreader (such as Outlook Express). Most of the newsgroups on the server are also copied to other news servers, so you may already have access. The Word newsgroups all start with *microsoft.public.word*, and there are groups on most Word topics.

> *msnews.microsoft.com*

Microsoft Template Gallery
> A site supplying templates for many situations and for most of the Office products, including Word.

> *http://officeupdate.microsoft.com/templategallery/default. asp*

Books

Word 2000 in a Nutshell, Walter Glenn, O'Reilly & Associates
> A compact reference that uncovers all of Word's documented and undocumented features and shares powerful time-saving tips. Look for an updated version in 2003.

Word Power Tools, Westley Annis, O'Reilly & Associates
> Describes many little-known techniques for getting the most out of Word. Forthcoming in 2003.

Writing Word Macros, Steven Roman, O'Reilly & Associates
> Shows you how to use VBA to automate all the tedious, repetitive jobs you never thought you could do in Microsoft Word.

Word 2000 Developer's Handbook, Guy Hart-Davis, Sybex
  A huge work documenting the intricacies of using VBA in the Word environment.

Word Tools

WOPR
  WOPR (Woody's Office Power Pack) is actually several utilities created by Woody Leonhard. They include the WOPR Places Bar Customizer, WOPR Two-by-Four (for multi-page printing), and WOPR Power Pack (which includes many useful tools). There is no free trial for these products.

  http://wopr.com/html/woprexplained.shtml

CrossEyes
  Powerful utility that lets you see a complete visual map of everything in a Word document in a single pane and in-line with the text, including direct formatting, styles, breaks, frames, and much more. Something like the Reveal Codes function in WordPerfect. Free trial.

  http://www.levitjames.com/

Stylizer
  Style utility that lets you search and apply paragraph styles by example, remove all existing formatting from a document, recreate documents with appropriate styles, and more. Free trial.

  http://www.levitjames.com/

DocWorks
  Add-in with tools for managing document lists, adding free-form notes to documents, and timing your work on a document. Free trial.

  http://www.office-power.com/products/

Shortcut Organizer
> Free add-in for copying custom keyboard shortcuts between documents, using a dialog structured like Tools → Templates and Add-Ins → Organizer.
>
> *http://www.chriswoodman.co.uk*

CDEV Word Tools
> Free collection that includes many small utilities, such as inserting random text, inserting address from Address Book, displaying table cell references in the status bar, and more.
>
> *http://www.cdev.co.uk/utils.htm*

Index

We'd like to hear your suggestions for improving our indexes. Send email to
index@oreilly.com.

Other Titles Available from O'Reilly

The Missing Manuals

Windows XP The Home Edition: The Missing Manual

By David Pogue
1st Edition May 2002
584 pages, ISBN 0-596-00260-2

This book begins with a tour of the Desktop and the new two-column Start menu, and tips for customizing the Taskbar and toolbars. Later chapters explore each control panel and built-in application, walk through every conceivable configuration, and show how to set up a small network and share a single Internet connection among several PCs. Finally, special chapters celebrate the standard rituals of Windows life: troubleshooting, installation, and upgrading.

Windows XP Pro: The Missing Manual

By Craig Zacker, Linda Zacker
& David Pogue
1st Edition January 2003
672 pages, ISBN 0-596-00348-X

Windows XP is the latest, most reliable, and best-looking version of the world's most widely used operating system, combining the extremely stable engine of Windows 2000 with the far superior compatibility of Windows Me. But one major failing of Windows remains unaddressed in the XP edition: It comes without a single page of printed instructions.

Photoshop Elements 2: The Missing Manual

By Donnie O'Quinn
1st Edition June 2003 (est.)
400 pages (est.), ISBN 0-596-00453-2

This guide carefully explains every feature that Abode's new photo editor has to offer by putting each one into a clear, easy-to-understand context. Author Donnie O'Quinn tells consumers which features of Photoshop Elements 2.0 work well, which don't, and why. O'Quinn doesn't just point out how to straighten photos, crop, and adjust the lighting, contrast, color and focus. He also offers a collection of tips and tricks for using Elements features, from the most basic selection to the most advanced color correction, and from classic darkroom techniques to stylized digital effects.

Windows 2000 Pro: The Missing Manual

By Sharon Crawford
1st Edition November 2000
450 pages, ISBN 0-596-00010-3

In *Windows 2000 Pro: The Missing Manual*, best-selling Windows NT author Sharon Crawford provides the friendly, authoritative book that should have been in the box. It includes detailed guidance for installing, removing, and troubleshooting new software and hardware; exploring basic networking and Internet survival; and info on Windows 2000's local-management options—security, user profiles, backing up, and so on—all crowned by a beefy troubleshooting guidebook.

O'REILLY®

To order: *800-998-9938* • *order@oreilly.com* • *www.oreilly.com*
Online editions of most O'Reilly titles are available by subscription at *safari.oreilly.com*
Also available at most retail and online bookstores.

Switching to the Mac: The Missing Manual

By David Pogue
1st Edition March 2003
447 pages, ISBN 0-596-00452-4

David Pogue explains how Windows users can make a relatively trouble-free switch to Mac OS X. Novices and power users alike will learn how to move their files; adapt to Mac versions of programs such as Microsoft Office, FileMaker, Photoshop and Quicken; find familiar controls in the new system; set up a network to share files with PCs and Macs; and adapt their old printers, scanners, and other peripherals.

Power Users

PC Hardware in a Nutshell, 2nd Edition

By Robert Bruce Thompson
& Barbara Frichtman Thompson
2nd Edition June 2002
816 pages, ISBN 0-596-00353-6

Fully updated and expanded, *PC Hardware in a Nutshell*, 2nd Edition is a comprehensive guide to buying, building, upgrading, troubleshooting and repairing Intel-based PCs. Features include how-to advice for specific components, ample reference material, and a complete case study for building a PC using separate components. Although this book serves a number of audiences, from novice to expert, its focus is often on professionals who service and support computers frequently.

Word 2000 in a Nutshell

By Walter Glenn
1st Edition August 2000
520 pages, ISBN 1-56592-489-4

Word 2000 in a Nutshell is a clear, concise, and complete reference to the most popular word-processing program in the world. This book is the first choice of the Word power user who needs help completing a specific task or understanding a command or topic. It's also an invaluable resource that uncovers Word 2000's undocumented features and shares powerful time-saving tips.

O'REILLY®

To order: *800-998-9938* • *order@oreilly.com* • *www.oreilly.com*
Online editions of most O'Reilly titles are available by subscription at *safari.oreilly.com*
Also available at most retail and online bookstores.

Windows XP in a Nutshell

By David A. Karp, Tim O'Reilly
& Troy Mott
1st Edition April 2002
640 pages, ISBN 0-596-00249-1

Here is a book for the power user who is familiar with a previous version of Microsoft Windows and wants to go deeper into the system than the average Windows user does. Rather than a beginner's guide or tutorial, this straightforward reference delivers more than 500 pages of concentrated information. For those who are ready to customize the system or take on daily troubleshooting, *Windows XP in a Nutshell* will unlock the hidden power of Windows XP.

Dreamweaver MX: The Missing Manual

By David McFarland
1st Edition November 2002
792 pages, ISBN 0-596-00349-8

Dreamweaver MX: The Missing Manual is the ideal companion to this complex software. The book begins with an anatomical tour of a web page, and then walks users through the process of creating and designing a complete web site. Armed with this book, both first-time and experienced web designers can easily use Dreamweaver to bring stunning, interactive web sites to life. In addition, users new to database-driven web sites will be given an overview of the technology and a brief primer on using this new functionality in Dreamweaver.

Windows XP Annoyances

By David A. Karp
1st Edition October 2002
586 pages, ISBN 0-596-00416-8

This book is not here to complain or to criticize. Rather, the mission of *Windows XP Annoyances* is to acknowledge the problems and shortcomings of the latest Windows operating system-and the software that runs on it-in an effort to overcome them. Complete with a collection of tools and techniques, this book allows users to improve their experience with Windows XP and establish control of the machine-rather than the other way around.

O'REILLY®

To order: *800-998-9938* • *order@oreilly.com* • *www.oreilly.com*
Online editions of most O'Reilly titles are available by subscription at *safari.oreilly.com*
Also available at most retail and online bookstores.